ON OVERGROWN PATHS

CURRENT AMERICAN EDITIONS
OF WORKS BY KNUT HAMSUN

Dreamers (New York: New Directions)
Growth of the Soil (New York: Random House)
Hunger (New York: Farrar, Straus and Giroux)
Hunger (New York: PenguinPutnam)
On Overgrown Paths
(København and Los Angeles: Green Integer)
Pan (New York: Farrar, Straus and Giroux)
Pan (New York: PenguinPutnam)
Rosa (Los Angeles: Sun & Moon Press)
Under the Autumn Star (Los Angeles: Sun & Moon Press)
Victoria (Los Angeles: Sun & Moon Press)
Wayfarers (Los Angeles: Sun & Moon Press)
The Women at the Pump (Los Angeles: Sun & Moon Press)

Forthcoming

A Wanderer Plays on Muted Strings
(København and Los Angeles: Green Integer)
The Last Joy (København and Los Angeles: Green Integer)

KNUT HAMSUN

On Overgrown Paths

*Translated from the Norwegian
by Sverre Lyngstad*

GREEN INTEGER
KØBENHAVN & LOS ANGELES
1999

GREEN INTEGER
Edited by Per Bregne
København/Los Angeles

Distributed in the United States by Consortium Book
Sales and Distribution, 1045 Westgate Drive, Suite 90
Saint Paul, Minnesota 55114-1065

First Green Integer edition 1999
English language translation ©1999 by Sverre Lyngstad
©1949 by Gyldendal Norsk Forlag
Published originally as *På gjengrodde stier*
(Oslo: Gyldendal Norsk Forlag, 1949).

This book was published in collaboration with
The Contemporary Arts Educational Project, Inc.,
a non-profit corporation, through a matching grant from
the National Endowment for the Arts, a federal agency.

NATIONAL
ENDOWMENT
FOR THE
ARTS

Design: Per Bregne
Typography: Guy Bennett

LIBRARY OF CONGRESS CATALOGING IN PUBLICATION DATA
Hansun, Knut [1859–1952]
On Overgrown Paths
ISBN: 1-892295-10-5
p. cm — Green Integer 22
I. Title II. Series III. Translator

It's the year 1945.

On the 26th of May the Arendal[1] chief of police came to Nørholm and proclaimed house arrest for my wife and myself for thirty days. I had not been notified. My wife handed over my firearms to him as requested. I had to write the chief of police afterward that I also had two large pistols from the latest Olympic Games in Paris; he could pick them up at his convenience. In the same letter I wrote that surely the house arrest was not to be taken literally, considering I had fields that needed to be looked after at great distances from the house.

Some time later the sheriff's assistant in Eide township came and picked up the two pistols.

*

On the 14th of June I was taken by car from my home and brought to the hospital in Grimstad[2]—my wife had been picked up a few days earlier and taken to the women's prison in Arendal. Now, of course, I could no longer look after the farm. That was very unfortunate, inasmuch as a mere youth was left in charge of it all for the time being. But it couldn't be helped.

At the hospital I was asked by a young nurse if I would like to go to bed right away—there had been a story in *Aftenposten*[3] to the effect that I had suffered "a breakdown and required care." "Bless you, child, I'm not sick," I said. "Never did anyone enter a hospital more fit than I, it's just that I'm deaf!" She may have taken it for a boast, and she refused to engage in conversation with me. Yes, she refused to speak to me, and this silence was observed by all the nurses during my stay in the hospital. The sole exception was the head nurse, Sister Marie.

*

I wander about the hospital grounds. A quite old building up on a hill and a more recent building down below—the hospital proper. I live on the hill, alone; the three young nurses live on the second floor. There's no one else in the house.

I'm taking a look around. There are many large oaks to be seen nearby, but many were also felled in bygone days, and from the stumps there now grows a wild oak scrub that will never amount to anything. The view shows many small farms to the west.

The policeman who drove me here said that I must not step "outside this room." Again, this was surely not to be taken literally, but I would like to be an obedient probationary prisoner and haven't ventured even a stone's throw away. Strange to think, by the way, that I who never had anything to do with the police in any country, as much as I roamed about the world—well, I had after all set foot in four of the five continents—should now, in my old age, have been arrested. Well, if it ever was to happen, it would have to happen now, before I died.

*

I wander about day after day. The three young nurses—student nurses actually—spell one another climbing the hill with food for me, turn on their heels and disappear. "Thanks a lot!" I shout after them. It gets a bit lonesome, but I'm used to being alone; even at home they don't speak to me, because I'm so deaf and tiresome. When I've eaten, I carry the tray with the empty dishes out into the hallway where they can be picked up.

Afterward I must either go out again or play a game of solitaire. I didn't manage to bring any reading, and my newspapers haven't arrived. After a few days I ask the young girl, "I saw that the mailman was here, weren't there any papers for me?"

To my delight she answers, and she answers loud and clear, but she says, "You aren't allowed to read newspapers!"

"I see. Who said that?"

"The chief of police in Arendal."

"Really. Many thanks."

But the head nurse finds a remedy for this by letting me rummage in a cabinet of old books and vintage newspapers. These are things that have been given to the hospital by benevolent people—schoolbooks, magazines for children and juveniles, bound newspaper serials, *For Rich and Poor, The Santal, The Evangelist,*[4] and in the midst of all this a gem: a book by Topsøe.[5]

I resolve to read sparingly to make it last longer, I have especially high hopes for several volumes of serials from the daily *Morgenbladet.*[6] I see they used

8

to belong to the library of Smith Petersen. This fellow Smith Petersen once lived in Grimstad and was a great magnate.

But in the teeth of my resolve to ration my reading, I pitched greedily into Topsøe's book and devoured it in one mouthful. Topsøe, whom Brandes[7] refused to write about. And now they are both dead.

*

A police officer comes and puts a number of questions to me and writes down my answers. It's of no interest to me. It seems to be important to the authorities to find out how much I own—there had been some talk in *Morgenbladet* about my "great fortune." I declared what I owned.

Then it was quiet for a few days, apart from the fact that a police officer came around with a "Resolution on Administration of Property" and another officer with a "Declaration of Public Indictment."

"I wish I owned that fine bicycle you've got," I say.

"Won't you read the declaration?" he says.

"Well, not exactly."

*

9

On June 23rd I was brought before the examining magistrate.

He immediately met me with a half smile: "You surely must have more money than you have declared?"

I was dumbfounded and looked at the man. "I haven't set much store by money," I said.

"All right, but still."

"My assets are what I have declared: about 25,000 in cash, 200 shares in Gyldendal Publishers, and the farm Nørholm."

"Right. But what about your copyrights?"

"Well, if Your Honor can give me an opinion about them today, I would be very grateful. My prospects as a writer do not look very promising right now."

Good Lord, how I must have disappointed him. And how I disappointed all the others who had hoped to poke their noses into my "great fortune." Not that my fortune isn't great enough, all too great. I have no desire to take it with me to the grave.

The hearing was decorous and indecisive. To several of the magistrate's questions I replied evasively in order not to needlessly irritate the well-meaning gentleman. Judge Stabel[8] is fanatical in his hatred of Germany, and he believes like a grain of mustard seed in the Allies' noble, unadulterated right to destroy the German nation and raze it from the face of the earth. Besides what has already been made public from the hearing, I will mention a couple of minor things.

He asked me what I thought of the company of National Socialists I had fallen in with here in Grimstad.

I answered that there were better people than I among that company. But I kept to myself that there were no fewer than four physicians, to mention just one category.

It sounded as if I was altogether too good to be part of the Nazi conspiracy.

"There were also judges," I said.

"Yes, unfortunately." And what did I make of the German atrocities in Norway, which had now been brought to light?

Since the chief of police had forbidden me to read the papers, I knew nothing about that.

Didn't I know about the murders, the terror, the torture?

"No. I heard some rumors just before I was arrested."

"Well, a wretch named Terboven,[9] who got his orders directly from Hitler, tortured and butchered the Norwegian people for five years. But thank God, the rest of us stuck it out. Do you think the Germans are a civilized nation?"

I didn't answer.

He repeated the question.

I looked at him and didn't answer.

"If I were chief of police, I'd let you read all the papers. Your case is postponed until September 22."

*

Three months, that is.

I read, ramble, and play solitaire.

To exercise my legs a bit within the restricted area allotted me, I scramble up the hill. It's very steep, and here and there I have to hang on with a sharp stick so as not to slide down to the bottom again. And that's not all: I get so outrageously dizzy that I feel like vomiting and have to force myself to swallow. I probably started too late with my mountain climbing. I repeat the walk day after day and am getting better at it, but I tremble all over once I've made it up.

On the top there is a flat area. Sitting up here, I see a couple of lighthouses, the ship's channel to Grimstad, and a few miles out along the Skagerrak. At first I have to sit still, not daring to get up and put on airs; but my brain ticks and works. I look at my watch—oh dear, I've used only a few miserable minutes for my climb, and here I sit on my pinnacle feeling pleased with myself, as if I had accomplished something. In order to make a hike of it I have to figure out a way of getting down the other side of the hill and sneaking back to the hospital unseen.

It works out, I get down very handily. But here I bump into a road, and I don't dare go this way and perhaps meet someone. And when I look at my watch, I haven't yet had anything like a hike—I simply have to turn around and walk over the hill once more.

That, too, was no problem for me, though I did take a stupid fall, with my arm caught under me. And I managed the steep descent to the hospital by sitting on a layer of leafy twigs and sliding.

Indeed, the whole thing was not at all badly conceived and executed by me, if I may say so. And I made no changes in these walks later on. The only fear I had was that a policeman might come looking for me at the hospital during my absence.

But when, days or weeks later, I came to reflect on the benefits of these walks over the hill, I was not very satisfied. It wasn't the right exercise for my muscles and limbs, it cost me too much strain, I grew sweaty and dog-tired without my body limbering up. My feet still felt wilted under me. Besides, my shoes hadn't borne up under the stress, both the uppers and the soles were torn. And I had no other shoes.

The head nurse is to be seen very seldom. She has too little help and must do the cooking herself. But once when she showed herself, she told me straightaway that I should walk about more. She pointed out a fairly long road to Smith Petersen's burned-down villa and said I should walk there.

"I'll take your word for it, Sister. Many thanks."

It was a great help, I could walk as fast or slow as I pleased. And there was a little dog on one of the farms who watched for me each time and came up happily to greet me.

At the same time I didn't want to completely give up my walks over the hill either. I had dreamed them up myself, there were trees and rocks that I recognized, and I knew there was a friendly rustle around me, even though I was deaf and could no longer hear it.

*

I sit at a crossroads holding a postcard in my hand. I have written home to Nørholm on the card, asking if they would try to find some shoes for me, and now I'm waiting for someone who is going to town and can take the card with him.

The very first to come is a young boy, maybe sixteen or so. He has a dark, unattractive face, but I get up, hold the card out and say, "Would you be so kind as to drop this card into a mailbox for me?"

The boy winces, his whole face becoming distorted, and long before I've finished speaking I hear a grumble and see him continue on.

"Maybe you aren't going to town?" I shout extenuatingly.

He doesn't answer, just walks on.

Having been so unlucky with my first appeal, I

don't dare make another try and walk back to the hospital.

*

There can be no doubt that this young boy knew me. He knew very well that I was in custody, and now he was going to demonstrate his proud posture vis-à-vis that sort of creature.

We now have political prisoners in Norway. Before our time the political convict was, for us, only a sort of fantasy in Russian books; we never saw him, the whole concept was unknown to us. The Thrane trouble, Kristian Lofthus, Hans Nielsen Hauge[10] do not count. But today we have one who does count—he roams the land of Norway in droves, as many as forty, fifty or sixty thousand specimens, people say.[11] And perhaps many thousand more.

Let that be as it may.

People associate the political prisoner with something criminal—he's probably carrying a machine gun, beware his sheath knife, children and young people must be particularly vigilant. I have noticed it during these weeks and months, it has been such a touching sight. Anyway, what harm would it have

16

done the young man if he had been polite and accepted my postcard? It's no skin off my nose, that's true. But for me to get a card mailed is fraught with such uncertainty. The young nurses going to town would rather not be bothered, which is quite understandable. And the mailman refuses to take anything.

I read, ramble and play solitaire.

*

Apropos the sheath knife. A sheath knife has found its way to my room, I don't know how. A fine knife, with engraved German-silver ferrules and a leather sheath. I ask the man who sweeps the yard, but it's not his. I guess I'll have to ask the head nurse.

A gentleman dressed in gray summer clothes comes to my room, nods and says nothing. Maybe he assumes that I know him, but I don't. Then I gather that he mumbles he is a doctor and says his name. I don't hear anything and have to ask him to repeat it—"Erichsen?" But I know only one Doctor Erichsen, and he's supposed to be in custody, I've heard. The stranger looks for something in his wallet, maybe his card, doesn't find it and gives up. There we are.

"Do you want something of me?" I ask.

He shakes his head, and I understand that he just wants to say hello.

I thank him. "It is very kind of you. Otherwise I associate mostly with the police these days—I'm a prisoner, you know, a traitor to his country—"

"How are you getting on here?" he asks.

"Just fine."

Shortly afterward he left. He was very friendly, but he didn't speak loud enough for me.

*

For that matter, there is no lack of people who are friendly. A shortcut, a path, runs up to my hill, and many take this path in preference to going around by the hospital proper. I come here now and then because it has such good places for sitting in dumb quietude, observing the ants and growing wise. Then people pass by, and some of them say hello. They know the reason why I'm sitting here, but they say hello.

An elderly lady stops one day and looks at me. I

get up and tip my hat. She starts talking, I say I can't hear, but she just talks. Then she points up at the sky, and I nod. She points again and again up at the sky, as if I too might have a chance, and I nod. She stops another lady coming by, and both ladies agree and give me their hands when they leave. Pure friendliness.

And I—in my thoughtlessness I forgot to give them my postcard to take along!

I shake my head at myself and climb the steepest part of the hill for punishment. I really have to get down to serious business now, for my shoes are more torn than ever. They are some eight years old and stem from the year I was in Serbia.

I had gotten to the other side of the hill and continued walking till I could see the church tower. By now I was obviously on forbidden ground, but if I stole far enough—and still a wee bit further—I could check my watch by the tower clock. However, the real reason for my being here was to look around for a mailbox.

On my right was a street without a soul. I began to walk down this street, but of course I was scared, so I walked on tiptoe. All the way down I caught sight of Grefstad's Hardware Store, and on the outside was a mailbox.

Should I be brazen? It all hangs on a few steps. I steal a glance around, but there's not a soul to be seen. Next I run like a streak across the street, drop my postcard into the box and run like a streak back again. Then I start walking.

I hadn't got far up the hill before I felt a nudge in my back. Police. Foolish and irritable as I had become these last few weeks, I was terribly startled.

"I just want to tell you that the tower clock is twenty minutes late," I say. "Do you have a watch on you?"

He fumbles in his pocket for his watch and we compare times.

"But that won't help you any," he says. "You aren't allowed to walk in the streets. How could you think of such a thing?"

I explain everything, just a postcard, a few words. "Here, just take a look at my shoes!"

"We're talking about two different things," he says.

"We certainly are," I say. "And I beg your pardon. By the way, weren't you the one who drove me to the hospital some time ago?"

"No," he replies curtly. "But it doesn't matter who it was."

"Certainly. But it's just that I simply had to send the little postcard I went to the mailbox with."

"Now look here," he says. "You are required to stay in the hospital, and I don't want to see you again in the middle of town. You understand?"

"Yes," I say. "I'm just thinking how unlucky I was. After all, I could've waited a moment and given the postcard to you, and you would've put it in the mailbox and it would all have been legal."

He looks at me a moment and says, "I won't report you this time. But now you'll take yourself off, right this minute. Get lost!"

*

What wonderful serials *Morgenbladet* used to run in the old days! I have no idea what they are like now, but in Smith Petersen's time the choice of literature was done with discernment, and I couldn't wish for any better reading today. The problem is that they take almost no time at all, even if they run to hundreds of pages. I've got a houseful of books in my yard back home, and I could get a truckload brought here now and then; but can you imagine, my money has been taken into custody along with me! It doesn't bother me; I just smile, toadying to no one. A nice lady in Java has sent me a box of cigars via Holland, she and her husband have read some of my books, she says, kind regards and thanks. How wonderful of her to do that, I think to myself, being a foreigner and so far away, bless her! People favor the old. But some day I will be out of cigars, what then? Then I'll quit smoking, just quit. I've done it three times before, for one year each time, to the day. I'm going to have that much control over myself as to quit. Good. But of course I'll start again, so what is it all for? I'm also going to have that much control of myself as to start again.

And I have no intention at all of putting my candle under a bushel.

*

Nothing much happens in my daily round right now. An old man comes up the hill with a coffin on his handcart, his old wife walks behind pushing. This is the second time since I arrived that the old couple come this way with a coffin. Someone died in the hospital last night; the body is placed in an out-building here on the hill until it is buried. Quietly and peacefully, nothing very special. He unties the rope, goes to the head end and pulls. The wife gives another push, and the coffin slides nicely onto the floor.

"You wouldn't be the one who left a sheath knife lying around, would you?" I ask.

"A sheath knife?" I believe he says; for I can see that he runs his hands over his clothes. Then he shakes his head.

A stream of talk follows, he wants to know more about the knife: What was it like, how did it look? I go my way, as though I just remembered I have to take care of something in my office.

And I really do. As a matter of fact, I'm not idle; like everybody else in these times I have to darn my socks every day and mend the sleeve of my jacket at the elbow. And then there are so many small tasks that I won't even mention: I must make my bed, smoke my morning cigar and swat flies. I must fasten a chair leg that is constantly falling out and drive a nail into the wall for my hat—I've already found myself a stone to do it with. Finally, I should also answer a certain letter that arrived last month, but I'm no writer and let it go.

It has all got to be done.

There is less to say about my environs. Here there's nothing but a bald hill without a flower bed. The weather is nippy, the wind almost always a gale; but nearby are trees and woods with songbirds aloft and all kinds of crawling things on the ground. Ah, the world is beautiful here too, and we should be very grateful to be part of it. There is a wealth of color even in rock and heather, the ferns have wonderful forms, and I still have a nice taste in my mouth from a bit of polypody that I found.

Now a plane flies over the hill and stirs things up, now there are two cows tethered down the hill. I feel sorry for them the way they stand there; I can see they are bellowing, impatient because they don't get moved and watered.

When the time comes there is food for me. One of the three young nurses pushes a tray onto my table, turns on her heel and leaves. "Many thanks!" I call after her. No, the three nurses do not change their tactics. They probably have a rough time getting up the hill without the coffee or soup spilling over. I don't know. But the tray is a mess. That's the way it should be, I've got it coming to me. At the beginning of my stay here I tried to explain to them that I hadn't killed anyone, stolen anything, or set fire to a house, but it didn't make any impression on them, they were bored. Now I don't explain anything anymore, it's nothing to make a fuss over. Soup by itself, coffee by itself—granted, that wouldn't be so bad either. But now I fish a letter out of the tray, it has been opened and sealed again. The police sent it that way. Or it is a clipping from a Swedish newspaper. Or a charming Danish actress sends me her regards. When I have fished it out of the tray, I dry it in the sun. It's good that way too. But I feel sorry for the three nurses, young and pretty all three, but so badly brought up.

*

There is a legend about Smith Petersen's burned-down villa. It's said to have been quite a sight, and a place for excursions.

First, I come upon a wooden bridge without a railing, barely more than a ford; but then I stop at some huge ash trees, hundreds of years old and majestic, only five or six altogether, no more, the rest must have died. I work my way up a neglected stony road and reach the ruins.

The villa was of wood, the remaining walls suggest a small, ordinary country house with extensions and additions as they were needed. I cannot get myself to believe that this was anything to boast about, but it may, of course, have contained an inner greatness, with coziness and comfort, splendor and luxury and earthly glory, what do I know. And there could have been festivities and grand moments and fantastic nights, which live on in the legend. Here was the dynasty of Smith Petersen, some members hyphenated, others not. One Smith Petersen was a consular agent in Grimstad, they still talk about Smith Petersen's wharf.[12] I know nothing about any of them, I only had a letter from a certain Smith Petersen once, in a sadly illegible hand. Wasn't he the French consul? He probably drove with a pair and had a coachman with shining buttons, and that was a great deal in those days; now he would have had two limousines and been forced to build a proper road up to his place.

But that's not what I'm trying to fathom, but

this: that so few things last. That even dynasties give way. That even what is grandiose falls some day. There is no pessimism in this thought or reflection, only a recognition of how non-stagnant, how dynamic life is. Everything is in motion, bubbling over with vitality, up and down and to all sides; when one thing collapses something else rises, looks large in the world for a moment and dies. *The Sayings of the High One* in the Poetic Edda expresses a belief in an innocent, static permanence of fame. But from Madagascar we have a saying among the natives: Tesaka doesn't like things which last!

Oh, those cackling hens of Madagascar, they will have their way!

We human beings aren't that wise, we refuse to give up the illusion of permanence. Flying in the face of God and fate, we try to force our way to fame and immortality, kissing and stroking our own folly, withering down to the roots without style or poise.

I see in my mind's eye a drawing by Engström[13] from fifty years back: A hoary couple sit dozing on a garden bench. It's fall. The man has a long stubble. His hands hold on to a stick.

They mumble the following conversation:

27

"I remember a girl called Emily."

"But my dear, that was me."

"Oh, was it you?"

Bjørnson[14] was aware of his transience: time takes it all! So what do the rest of us have to say! For my own part, I sit making notes, scribbling about a burned-down wooden villa and having my own thoughts about the affair. Over at the nearest farm a little dog is running back and forth—I can see it's barking at me, but I'm not distracted by it. I'm at peace, my mind is clear and my conscience free. I receive letters to the effect that I will be read for ages, even patriots[15] brag about me. Let it be as it may with such kindness. In any case, few things last, time takes them, time takes all and everything. I lose a bit of my name in the world, a portrait, a bust—there would scarcely have been an equestrian statue anyway.

But something else is worse—even to talk about. I had thought I was on good terms with children. They would come now and then with their little books for me to write my name in, and they curtsied and thanked me, and we were all happy together. Now I'm used as a boogeyman for children.

Let that be as it may, too. In a hundred years, perhaps less, the children's names will be forgotten, together with my own.

*

I cannot understand what sort of person it could have been who bought Topsøe's book and took it with him to the hospital. I've been pondering this for a few days. And now, when I try to get hold of the book again, it's gone.

Gone!

Who has taken it? It's no use asking, I won't get an answer, at most they will say, "Don't know!" I would have examined the book carefully, page by page, looking for an eventual mark; I'm sorry I didn't do it right away, and now it's too late. It was a nice unused copy, but it might well have been bought fifty or a hundred years ago—I have lost count of the years, and I have nothing to look them up in.

In my younger days I met the Topsøe family in Paris, but only the wife and three young children, Topsøe himself having died. A handsome and endearing family with higher interests; one daughter played the violin, I believe another studied art, none of it was in my line.

But the patient who one day came to Grimstad Hospital with one of Topsøe's books in his hand, who was he? In my idleness and indolence I do a bit of playacting to myself, pretending it is very important to discover this secret; in reality it doesn't interest me in the least. And I said as much to myself, not mincing my words: it's just some nonsense, even worse than crossword puzzles and solitaire, and don't you think I know it!

Whereupon I set about washing some clothes to make myself useful. There's no warm water, but I've got soap with me and am anything but helpless; I know the trick from my youthful days on the prairie, where we didn't have any warm water either.

Suddenly there is a knock on the door. I'm half undressed, but say "Come in!" It's a lady, a young girl. "What in the world!" I can't help blurting out. For not only do I stand there naked from the waist up, I don't even have my teeth in place.

She moves her lips. She is pale and embarrassed.

"I can't hear you, miss."

She writes on a paper, "I beg your pardon for taking this book away from you."

"What book? Topsøe? It's not my book."

"I picked it up here yesterday, from your table."

"I see. Well, I found it in the hallway cabinet. It's a Danish book."

"Yes. Marvelous!" she wrote. "I didn't know that someone named Topsøe ever existed."

In the meantime I have managed to get dressed.

The lady writes, "I'm terribly sorry! I knocked on your door several times yesterday too, I really did. And then I walked in."

In my confusion I say, "I thought you were Danish."

She shook her head and wrote her name.

She told me she was staying at a small summer place on the coast. She and her mother. They went there every year. It was only a cottage on an island. But now, unfortunately, they had to leave.

"Why do you go around with pen and paper? Do you take notes when you read?"

She blushed and wrote, "I knew you were deaf."

"Won't you sit down, miss?"

She writes and writes—she has such pretty

hands, fine nails, a couple of rings on her left hand. Her face is without any sort of paint. She's young and natural, I mean to say innocent.

I begin to chat a little: "I have to laugh thinking how I looked when you came in, some idea it must have given you! You see, I have to do a bit of washing now and then; I could send it home, of course, but it takes so much time. A pair of shoes which I've been trying so hard to get from home came only today."

"I'm so sorry!"

"No, no, I just laugh it off. It will pass."

"That's just like you! Sometimes at home we all laugh when we read something jolly you've written! But sometimes—"

"Are you many at home?"

"There's only my sister, but she's married and has her own home. Then there's Father, Mother and me."

"Isn't your father with you on the island?"

"No. Not this year. He's been arrested."

Pause.

"It was nice of you to come see me."

"No. We knew very well that you wouldn't want

it. But you see, we'll be leaving now, and so I was sent. By the whole family. Ha-ha," she laughed.

"Oh yes, it was nice of you. True, I'd rather not have anyone come, but that's only generally speaking. I'm deaf, you know, and nobody has the patience to talk with me, and so I have forgotten myself how to talk to people."

"I wonder if you really are completely deaf. May I try?"

She spoke slowly and softly into my left ear, said a few trivialities and then looked questioningly at me."

"Yes," I say and nod.

"Did you really hear?"

"Yes, every word, I think. How could you know that my left ear is the best?"

"Because you turn your left side toward me when you listen. I noticed that."

We talked together, and she didn't write anymore. I praised her keen observation, and she told me she had begun to study nursing. I thanked her for coming—oh, I blessed her! "That I'll tell at home!" she said.

She looks for something in her handbag, finds it and offers it to me. "From Mother," she said, "it's yarn, something for darning. Yesterday I saw a sock you had started on, with the needle in it, it was lying there on the bed—"

"Well?"

"Oh, but you mustn't take it amiss," she said, "please! I don't usually go snooping about that way—"

"Oh, my dear child."

"I really don't. But I noticed that you had darned the wool sock with linen thread."

"Well, I'm not fully trained."

"But you probably don't have—. Mother thought that perhaps you didn't have any wool yarn."

"Oh yes, but I forgot. I can get as much as I want."

"Where? You can't buy that now."

What an imp! She's got me stumped and I have to say: "Please, thank your mother for me. But it's much too kind of her. I've never heard the likes, wool yarn these days!"

Sure, we talk together and it works out. But it requires a certain sacrifice on her part: she has to be very close to my ear. She says she's glad she met me today, because tomorrow they have to leave. I say I'm grateful that she came and feel very sad that she's leaving. "Really?" she asks. "That, too, I'll tell at home!"

When she had gone I sat there by myself, ruminating. A wonderful encounter for me. An audible silence now she's gone. And there on the table lies Topsøe's book, as much of a mystery as before; but I no longer care to know who owned it in the previous century. There is nothing like feeling the breath of living life.

*

September 2. A policeman comes into my room and says without any introduction, "You're going to move."

"Really. So where am I going?"

"To Landvik."

The head nurse also turns up and says Landvik. I ask what sort of place in Landvik. To that I get no answer, but the head nurse explains that the hospital will now be receiving polio patients and my room will be occupied.

I thank her for my stay and for the loan of all the books, which I've now finished reading. Then I pack my suitcase and get in with the driver.

I ask no more questions about what place in Landvik, it doesn't matter to me where we're going. We turn into a little stub of a side road, and going around a curve I read OLD PEOPLE'S HOME on a large white building.

So, that was why the head nurse and the policeman were so secretive, they didn't want to frighten me with the old people's home. But it just suits me fine, and I can't help smiling at their concern. I don't allow myself to be upset and take my time getting out. It's sheer affectation on my part. In reality, I'm rather bewildered at seeing so many old people in one place.

I greet the manager, a woman, get a room on the second floor, and wave goodbye to the police car. It's Sunday today and bright and sunny, hence all the people by the steps. I mingle with them all, but nobody speaks to me; nor would it have done any good, their new comrade is so deaf.

And here in the old people's home I take each day as it comes. My being here makes no difference one way or the other, but everything takes its course. Adventures? Great shocks? Far from it. Unless it can be called an experience to read about the complementary colors in Goethe's chromatology without understanding a word of it.

But I'm grateful to the police that I've come here, it's an ideal place for me. Here I can take long walks without hearing a word about town limits; I eat, sleep and read. I also write a little, but that I won't mention so as not to annoy anybody.

The old people's home is a big place, worthy of a big community. It has a municipal board room, various offices and a public library; it has daily mail delivery, telephone, radio, and many people coming and going about their business, and beyond the center the countryside. The most important office is probably that of the cashier, but the poor relief office boasts two young girls who sit there writing, two beauties in the midst of this incredibly hoary world of eighty- and ninety-year-olds.

Since I haven't been allowed to read the papers, I have done so on the sly. It was difficult for me in the hospital, but when I received laundry from home various papers were enclosed in a separate bundle, so I learned a little about what was going on, for the first time also about German atrocities in our country. There were, of course, big gaps in the information sent to me with the laundry in this way, but I wasn't a complete illiterate.

Here in the old people's home I have an easier time of it, I can read every number of the Grimstad paper in the kitchen, and that's a great help. On the whole everything is easier here. The manager is a sympathetic, good-humored lady who has been in charge of the home for twenty-three years, and though she's only half the age of some of us, she comes regularly around to her foster children with chocolate and candy and cake when the rations arrive. The only thing she hasn't obtained for me is the good will of the librarian. That she can't manage. A half-educated man, a teacher, he won't let me take out any of the books in the public library.

Even though I may have written some of them. I don't know.

*

When I take my walks I put my back into it, so that I won't have anything to reproach myself with. I do it for the sake of my nights, in order to earn my sleep. Sleep is better than food, there's no comparison. Oh, don't get the idea that sleep is to sit shoveling food into my mouth! Sleep is the wonderful madness of finding in my pocket some money I never lost and which I've been desperately looking for. Sleep is that I finally shake off a brawny sailor whom I am about to kill, but who in return pinches me with a pair of shears. Ah, what a wonderful thing sleep is, life and fable and miracle all at once.

But for all that, food can also be good for something, I won't deny it.

I have no set schedule, when it hits my fancy I pick up my staff and go. It doesn't come natural to me to use the staff very much, it just comes along like a dog, no more. Most people call my staff a stick, my walking stick: "Would you like me to fetch your walking stick?" they used to say to me in the hotels at one time. But that was too elegant, I think, so I always call it my staff. It is shaped like a crook and has a rubber tip, but unfortunately it also has an unsightly lashing of steel wire near the end, where it cracked. By the way, it has several marks indicating metric measurements, which make me self-sufficient should the need arise.

I say hello to the children I meet; some of the

boys must have heard that I'm deaf and amuse themselves by getting up close and screaming something at me. I also say hello to grownups if they seem to invite it, but if they are standoffish and turn away from me I walk by indifferently. But I'm ready to greet them, I can't deny it, I'm too ready to greet them. I was taught to do so in childhood, they said it was nice to greet people and it sticks with me still.

One sunny morning in Prague I was out looking for a cigar store. When I came inside a monk was standing there, the lady behind the counter was just handing him a coin; he thanked her and was about to leave. The scene was very strange to my Norwegian heart, and on the spur of the moment I added another coin. Overwhelmed, the monk began to say something, raising both his hands; I forgot my errand and didn't buy anything, just took myself off, out on the street and away. Afterward I walked around with love in my heart, for people and for this world of ours; I greeted everyone I met and they smiled back and greeted me in return. And nobody stopped me, it was all so beautiful. What people thought, what the street thought, I do not know—perhaps that I must be an early bird, since I was already returning from the tavern. What do I care! I am who I am, and Prague is a splendid city.

I read a long, long time ago—I'm so old that by now everything has happened many long years ago—I read a story about Socrates. He was walking with a friend on the street, and Socrates greeted someone they met. "He didn't answer!" the friend said indignantly. Socrates smiled and said, "It doesn't do me any harm that I'm more polite than he is."

So many things crowd in on me at this moment, things I could say in my defense, but I shall keep quiet about them. I could perhaps refer to the old-time Norwegians, who greeted one another by holding out their right hand to show they came unarmed. Or what about the time I stood beside the Japanese envoy in an Oslo elevator and we were both equally polite and neither would step out first? Nor do I regret getting up and giving my seat to a lady who got on a streetcar in Versailles. Then all the men got up, to be sure, but I was first. She was a handsome old lady in a widow's veil and with a string of pearls around her neck, perhaps a duchess of the blood, forsooth—she could have adopted me. Anyway, I gave those gentlemen, those Frenchmen, a lesson in courtesy which they won't forget, I was first.

Well, those were the days of my youth, which are of no interest now and therefore will not be mentioned. But even in Nordland,[16] in the bailiwick of Salten,[17] I remember we tucked our cap humbly underneath our left arm and said "Peace!" when we entered, "Godspeed!" to those who were working, and "Peace stay with you!" when we left.

That was our greeting.

*

Today, September 22, summoned once again before the examining magistrate.

It's early morning, a little too early for me and the entire old people's home. I could have been notified, but I was not; what are telephones for? Policemen don't have to worry, they can easily enough get into a car and go, but the prisoner has to come along just as he is. I would have liked to be ready and dressed when I was to appear before the examining magistrate. Even in czarist Russia they gave you time to catch your breath. Not here.

I mumbled an apology, and the fine old judge

pardoned me. Anyway, he didn't have very much on his mind: my appointed time was up today, and now it would be extended until November 23. It was explained, recorded and supported with sundry questions which the judge presented to me in writing to avoid speaking into my deaf ears. I answered one after another and affirmed my previous statement that I would answer for what I had done.

Then we were finished, and I was ready to ride back and put on some clothes.

*

Another two months—good, it makes no difference to me one way or the other. I don't really belong here in the old people's home, I am an intruder; but the old people are friendly and do not let me notice it. They have come here voluntarily as the most suitable place to live out their last days, while I have come here by courtesy of the police and am committed. The others may have their shortcomings as well, plagued by back problems or feeble legs, but I take the prize, being almost totally lacking in a certain sense and therefore no good for mumbling to. That's no small liability, and I have

43

many more: for example, I'm sometimes so desperately stuck for a word I want to use that, in order to say something, I have to say something else first. I'm not the only one suffering from this wearisome ailment, it's nice and old and is called aphasia; the great Swift in England had a worse case of aphasia than I.

But why grumble, everyone has his troubles. Nor does anything really matter here in the old people's home, we are free to come and go, to move about, to observe one another. We have a capacity crowd, fifteen, twenty, both genders, several bedridden. Now and then there is also someone who dies, it can't be helped, but it doesn't make much of an impression on the survivors. We follow the white coffin with our eyes, but when the hearse has driven off we turn back to ourselves again.

Come to think, isn't it a fashion of the day and time that the coffin has to be white now? I don't know what is most apropos, but in my childhood coffins were black, only children had white coffins. In other ways fashion or custom has changed according to the locale: around here flags are at halfmast all day for a dead body; in Nordland the custom was that, as soon as the coffin had been lowered into the grave, the flag was raised from half-mast to the top and stayed there.

Both ways may be good, perhaps equally good.

*

One day, as I'm jotting down some trifles for myself on my walk, a man catches up with me. It was a bit strange, because I had turned onto a remote forest trail away from all traffic and thought I couldn't be seen.

The man just barely smiled and began to keep in step with me. It suited me poorly and I tried to hang back. It didn't help. "I can't hear," I said. He nodded, and suddenly he managed to say something that was remarkably clear: "I know what sort of character you are!"

Slightly taken aback, I smiled at his embarrased attempt at a joke and said, "I'd rather walk alone."

The man didn't give up on me, he uttered some trivialities and I understood a word here and there.

He didn't have the looks of a thief, but he was a nuisance; I really felt like turning around and going my way, so I pretended to be reading what I'd written without bothering with him. But suddenly I heard him use an authentic expression from the Salten region: "Don't be sore about that!"

A recollection flashed through me at these simple words, my heart heard them. "Are you from Nordland?" I asked.

"Sure," he said. "But you don't know me."

Now he took turns addressing me in different ways, shifting from formal to familiar and vernacular speech, while taking pains to speak clearly, in short sentences and close to my ear. Perhaps it was the cadences of his voice that enabled me to understand most of it.

I won't say a word about his looks, he was so ordinary, all too ordinary: of medium height, a kindly face, thin and middle-aged. Maybe from want, maybe from humility, he carried his shoes tied together over his shoulder and walked barefoot.

"I'm glad I got to see you," he said.

Was there ever such a man! I could fairly grind my teeth.

"And that you're willing to listen to me," he said.

"I'm deaf, I have told you. What should I listen to?"

"We are both from Hamarøy."[18]

Well. I acted as if that was nothing special, but it made me much more amenable.

He handed me an almanac from several years back; it was in a worn leather binding, with lots of pages covered with writing that he asked me to read.

I had expected it, the story, his life.

"Isn't it getting too cold for walking barefoot now?" I asked to change the subject. "It will soon be October."

"I've written down everything truthfully," he said, wrapped up in his own thing.

Oh, how familiar it all was! Up to ten years ago I used to receive parcels in the mail with true-to-life local tales and love and poetry. "I can't read it," I said. "I'm not up to it."

"Since we're both from Hamarøy—"

"Where are you from there?"

"From Sagfjord,[19] from Kløttran."

"What's your name?"

"My name? Martin. I'm called Enevoldsen."

"I'll try to take a look at it," I said wearily, leafing through the volume. "But I can't read the whole thing, only here and there."

It told about a schoolmaster and a man named

Berteus; I saw the name Alvilde a couple of times, something about making one's peace with God, about going to Klingenberg,[20] and about a parson, fishing for a living, prospecting in the mountains—

No, I just couldn't read that way, with him standing there watching me. I handed back the volume to him, but I obviously couldn't get rid of this man just like that; in the end I didn't even have any desire to do so. He seemed to be imploring me, he was at my mercy.

We sat down in the heather and talked; I lighted my pipe, but he didn't smoke, he talked. I noticed that he was afraid of tiring me, and he pointed at the almanac and said, "You'd better read it yourself, Knut."

But I preferred to listen.

"Strange that I can hear you so well, Martin," I said, going along with his familiar mode of address. "Better than I've heard anyone else."

"I'm used to speaking clearly when I give my talks," he said.

"What sort of talks?"

"At prayer meetings."

"Oh, at prayer meetings." But it wasn't the words

I was thinking of, it was the sound, the tune. The tune of the words. His voice was not strong but made for my ear, and so it got through. Hearing him read verse with that voice might be thrilling.

"Do you recite hymns?" I asked.

"Oh no. Well, the psalms of David."

"And do you sing?"

"No. But I play the organ."

"So there was a girl called Alvilde?" I said of a sudden, looking at him.

He was surprised and answered, "Yes, she's called Alvilde. How come you know that?"

"I read it in your book."

"As you were welcome to do. Well, more than welcome! You did nothing wrong."

"But tell me, how did you get into this thing?"

"By the grace of God!" he replied.

"Well. But did you come straight from Kløttran on the Sagfjord and begin speaking at prayer meetings?"

"Oh no, no," he said helplessly. "It was the pastor who got me to do it. It was at a funeral that I first felt I had the call."

"And you spoke. What did you say?"

49

"I didn't say anything. I prayed to God. It was at Berteus's funeral. It's all written down there."

There was no help for it, he wouldn't let me off and I had to start reading. I didn't lose anything by that, far from it; the simple words and descriptions made for a good story and carried me away.

I read:

*

It began with there being a man named Berteus, he came from Kvædfjord[21] and settled down. He was married and they had a little one. He and I were so often together, though he was older and had been captain on a fishing boat. A fine man in every way and like a brother among brothers to me. He got lumber from Schøning's at Hillingen, and I lent him a hand when he built his house, and for that I got my board and didn't ask for anything more. In the fall he went back to Kvædfjord and sailed to Lofoten, he owned his own eight-oar. His wife stayed behind with us, in her new house. I won't say anything against her, but the little child was left alone in the house while she went berrying in the woods with the others. In the late winter they came rowing home with Berteus, he had typhoid and lay flat on his back for two days and nights. He was constantly wandering, and nobody wanted to stay with him because the typhoid was catching; not even his wife dared be with him lest the little one get hurt and catch it too, she said. And so it was I who sat with him, giving him sugar water with a feather that I wet his lips with, while he never stopped wandering. It lasted only two days and nights, then he was dead.

I was completely dazed when this happened, for we had all thought he would recover, but that was not to be. I didn't know how in the world to manage, how to reconcile myself to this sudden death; he was so hale and hearty when we built the house, and then he was called away! I lay brooding on it at night, I couldn't rest. His wife wanted to have him buried in the Kvædfjord cemetery, but it was too far out of the way, for his boat and crew had gone back to their fishing in Lofoten, and there was no other transportation to be had. Some good people rowed to Klingenberg for a coffin and a few provisions for the funeral, but I didn't go along. What if I too were summoned by death, just like Berteus, where would I then end up? The schoolmaster came and talked to me, saying I mustn't take it so hard, but to no avail. Then I scrambled through the snow up to a cliff called Eagle Crag, because it looks so much like an eagle, and there I went down on my knees and called upon God and Jesus in my distress. It did me good, I prayed for understanding and light for my soul, and verily my prayer was granted as never before. A long time went by, the sun moved down the sky, I saw several strangers down by the buildings, they had come back from Klingenberg with the coffin. It was then that I perceived a great clearness and an exceeding light within me, it was like the highest glory. I was quite beside myself and talked aloud all the way home without a break. The pastor had come and the body had been laid in the coffin; they were about to put the cover on and hushed me to be quiet, but the pastor waved to them, because he had confirmed me and knew me: "Let Martin be!" he said. I folded my hands and held them up high and prayed for mercy and forgiveness for Berteus's soul and for us all; I hardly knew what I was doing or how long I went on, until the pastor took my hand and thanked me. But when I sat down I went to sleep on my chair, exhausted. Glory to God in the highest! What I have written down here is about his good and faithful mercy toward me from that day on Eagle Crag until now.

Time passed and nothing more happened. The widow intended to go back to Kvædfjord and was waiting for the eight-oar and the crew to take her home. It was now April. What should she do with the house? She tried to sell it but couldn't, so she asked me to get the Sheriff to do it, and I promised I would. When I came back from the Sheriff she told me that I could have the house for the time being. I asked her what she meant. "I don't know what I mean," she said, "but, you know, you did help Berteus build the house, that's why I said it!" I still didn't understand what she meant. "No, you're thinking only about someone else," she said, "and she's making a big fool of you, because she's going to get together with the schoolmaster, you see!" "Yes, I know that," I said, "and now we won't talk any more about that but keep quiet." But the next day the eight-oar came to pick up her and the child, and she went back to her people in Kvædfjord where she had come from. Everything fell into place. Summer came, and the schoolmaster bought the house and moved in there and kept school. He got married at the height of summer and bought himself pots and pans and whatever else was needed at Klingenberg; they were a happy couple and lay in the hay and were content. The schoolmaster himself went week after week with a hammer in his hand prospecting in the nearby mountains, but he didn't find any precious metals that he could send in, and everything he had bought went down the drain; even the purchase of the house had to be annulled because he hadn't found anything in the mountains.

In late fall the schoolmaster got a better position in Helgeland[22] and went there; we missed him a lot, for he was a clever man and well versed in every field. He came from Tromsø Teachers College[23] bringing with him learning and insight, he could make up machines just like that, having it all in his head. You feel sorry for such a man. He taught me to play the organ and taught others different skills; his name was Hans Næss and he was a tall, handsome man, but he seemed to have difficulty

54

settling down to anything and forgot his God. He bought himself a farm in Helgeland, but that didn't turn out well either; after just a couple of years he had to give up the farm, and everything they owned was registered. Finally he decided he ought to go to America and that he really should have been there from the very beginning. On this point, other people felt he was right: for a man who knew as much as he did and could be so clever with his head and hands, America must be the only right place. He borrowed money for the ticket and got ready full of hope; I happened to be in Helgeland when he said goodbye to his family and set out. The only thing I could do was to pray a heart-felt prayer to God that he would fare well in his new life in the New World; finally I also prayed that the merciful Lord keep an eye on and protect his wife and the two little ones who were left behind here, but who were to follow as soon as the husband could afford it. And so he left. The Lord's will be done! She never saw him again.

No, she never saw him again in this world. She received a few letters from him saying he had arrived safely and was going west; after that he wasn't heard from. She read in the papers about a terrible fire in Chicago where so many were lost, so maybe he was among the casualties, or so she feared. But she never stopped making inquiries about him and thinking of him year after year, and besides she lived in the most wretched poverty. It was a hard time for her; she was neither married nor unmarried, and she had to provide for herself and her dear ones. Me she could barely endure the sight of when I came to those parts of the country, and she told me I would've done much better not to lend him the money for the ticket and thus bring disaster upon them all. I didn't know how to answer that and went away with sorrow in my heart. Seeing the state of mind she was in, I didn't dare show myself too often, but only sent her greetings at Christmas and the other holidays. This, too, made her sore at me, and the next time I came she was full of bitterness and told me many hateful things. "I can't understand why you come sneaking around to these parts," she said, "don't you have a home in Hamarøy?" "I just came from the south, and I'm on my way to the far north," I said, "so I just felt like dropping by." "No, you come sneaking around here," she said, "and what mustn't the people back home think? You don't imagine, do you, that you can make me forget the man you managed to get away from here? Ha-ha, my good Martin, you aren't offering yourself in his place, are you?" "No, that has not been my intention," I said. "Well, you just take away the things you've brought, I won't have them before my eyes," she said. "We don't need anything and you shouldn't go to any trouble!" "It was only a little something for the children," I said. "But I don't see why you can't keep away," she said. "I will keep away," I said.

I regretted saying that, for it only made matters worse and brought on tears. It was painful to watch. I told her I wasn't giving another thought to what she had said, but she called herself the worst scum and a louse and refused to be comforted. When I left she showed me out, crying all the while. "I suppose this is the last I'll see of you?" she said. "Don't use such sorrowful words," I replied, "next time perhaps you will have had some news. To God, nothing is impossible!"

*

I read no more and handed the almanac back to him. He was disappointed. That, too, was familiar to me: they don't understand how anyone can forbear reading all the rest, which is no worse than what has gone before, after all.

"So the schoolmaster came to grief," I said, to soothe him. "He married Alvilde, didn't he?"

He was taken aback. "It doesn't say that," he said. "No."

"There's no mention of that anywhere."

"Tell me now, have you spent all your days since youth speaking at prayer meetings?"

"I don't speak very much, I lack the learning for that. I pray to God."

"With all those years, it must be a lifetime."

"That's for sure. The time is gone and all the years are gone, I'm sorry to say, and yet I haven't done anything for us human beings on this earth."

"How did you get here, so far to the south?"

"Oh, I just go."

"By foot?"

"Yes. I walk. I've also been to Sweden and Finland."

"Pardon my asking," I said. "Do you get anything for it? I mean, does anyone pay you?"

58

"No. But God is merciful toward me, I suffer no want. Often I do a day's work and get a little for that; indeed, many times I have something left over. So I'm well taken care of."

"Do you just walk in and ask for something to eat?"

"No," he answered, shaking his head. "But when it falls out that way, I do get to eat with the others who are seated at table."

"I see. But when it doesn't fall out that way?"

"Well, then I wait until some other place, or I don't need anything. Anyway, it doesn't take very much."

I looked at the skinny wanderer and said, "I beg your pardon, but wouldn't it be better for you to join some association or religious community or society, so you could have something steady?"

"Yes, that may well be," he said. "But you see, I have no learning or knowledge I can show, so I have to go it alone and stick with God, that's the safest. Oh, it's easy for me to make my way, I pray to God and feel safe. When I enter a cottage or a home, I thank God that I've come under this roof and pray for heaven's blessing and forgiveness for us all. Usually there will be a few who come to listen, and if there is a small harmonium at hand, it turns into a regular hymn of thanksgiving. This is how it goes."

"Why is it so important to you that I read your almanac?"

"Oh well, there was a reason. Of course, I did hear about you now and then while growing up in Hamarøy, so I knew your name."

"But how did you know I was here?"

"I happened to hear of it from someone. And I decided right away that I would try to meet you."

"Oh, really."

"I heard that you'd become deaf, of course, but that didn't worry me much. My father was deaf and my mother was deaf, it was no use shouting at them, they didn't hear. There are also many people at the prayer meetings who are hard of hearing and never hear a word about God or a prayer to him."

"I see. And what did you think you wanted to meet me for?"

"Well, I can also tell you that, if you won't take it amiss?"

"No, no."

"Then I'll just say one word: that now you must

set your house in order. It's high time. You are an old man."

We both fell silent, and he said no more. No sermon—he had the good sense of not watering down his words. Maybe he had made up this parting word beforehand, maybe he was in the habit of using this word to old people he met on his way.

"Thank you for the trouble you've taken talking to me today," I said, sticking a small bill into his pocket.

But this made us both feel embarrassed, and to smooth it over I said, "Where will you be going from here?"

"Into town," he said.

"Then you must put on your shoes," I said.

"Yes, but there's no hurry," he said. "I'll save them till I find myself among people."

*

October has arrived. Naturally, I ran out of cigars quite a while ago, but it doesn't matter, I have tobacco in tins, Norwegian brand, and smoke my pipe. One day I see one of the old men come home with a tall tobacco plant, a regular shrub, which he has got hold of some place or other; he carefully plucks every dried little leaf from the stalk, stuffs his pipe with them and lights up. It works that way too, it works nicely, the rest of us oldsters perk up just from watching it. Since this summer, when I got better shoes from home, I haven't been short of anything. I've received a wonderfully hefty treatise on civilization from Denmark, and I managed to borrow a Bible right here, together with a big book about New Guinea.

One evening the doctor comes and says he's going to examine me.

"Why?" I ask.

"The police have been wondering whether you're going back to Nørholm, or whatever."

"Shall I get undressed?"

"No, not at all," he answers, "just unbutton your shirt a little."

He listened to my chest and my back. "Blood pressure a bit high perhaps," he said. "Would you like to go home?"

"I want what the police want. I have no will of my own now."

Finished. It had taken ten minutes.

I didn't attach much importance to this examination. The police seemed to me to be needlessly careful, I was hale and hearty. Blood pressure, what was that? Had never heard of it before. There was nothing the matter with me, I was just old and deaf.

Two days later a lawyer came with many big papers; he was supposed to draw up a list of my assets, he said. I declared the same as to the examining magistrate: 25,000 in cash, the farm Nørholm, and 200 shares in Gyldendal Publishers.

"But then there are the copyrights," he said, and put them down at 100,000.

Pure guesswork. I said, "They may be worth 100,000 kroner, they may not be worth 5 kroner, nobody knows, I'm a dead man. Ask at Gyldendal's, where they have professionals for this sort of thing."

He crossed out the 100,000 and put down 50,000 instead.

"Jewelry?" I thought he said.

Since I don't wear rings, I dived into my vest and was about to give him my watch, but he shook his head.

Finished.

A week went by. I was under the impression that

all was well, had visits from my daughter and daughter-in-law at Nørholm, joked and laughed with them, told them little things about my life. My relatives could tell me that I was now going to Oslo, to "a nice pension"; they had it from acquaintances in the police. Hmm, okay with me! I would be gone about a fortnight, the police had hinted. My relatives handed me each a packet of money, which I was to keep for them until I returned—this was something they used to do when they had got their hands on a few pennies.

The following evening the police came and drove me to Arendal. It was a Sunday. I entered an overcrowded railroad car and still knew nothing about the purpose of my journey—until the police in a most refined manner let fall into my hands an issue of *Aftenposten*, where it said that I was going to the Psychiatric Clinic. Secretiveness also here. When the train arrived in Oslo, I had been sitting straight up all night for twelve hours. And I was no youth. The boat would have taken seven hours, and I could have lain down.

It was on Monday morning October 15, between ten and eleven o'clock, that I was admitted, through

64

three locked doors, to the Psychiatric Clinic. And the three doors were locked behind me.

I was met by a swarm of white-clad nurses. I had to hand over everything I had in my pockets, my keys, my watch, a notebook, pocketknife, pencil, glasses, everything. I had two pins in my lapel, they were taken; my suitcase was stripped of its covering, probably for fear I might have hidden something dangerous underneath. Then they opened the suitcase and began to rummage among its contents.

A question came up about a report from the doctor. Didn't I have something in writing from the doctor? No. It was the police who had brought me, I was in custody; I was a traitor, they must know. The amiable head nurse asked me how such a misfortune could have befallen me. "It's no matter," I said. No, no, it was really too bad, such a pity. I said I would explain it all later.

They took me to the bath. I said I was hungry and tired, but they said I had to bathe. When I was getting into my clothes again, I couldn't find my tie pin. It had been removed from my tie while I was in the tub, and nobody said anything. I lay down

65

on the floor and looked for it, but no. I asked the attendant, no. I got angry and raised an outcry, hssh, hssh, hssh! I explained that it was an expensive little pin, an Oriental pearl, not to be confused with those big baubles which some went around with. Finally a nurse says that the pin has been taken care of.

And finally they gave me some tiny slices of bread that I began to munch on. While I was occupied with this, my name was called. I didn't understand what they were saying, and when I asked them to write it down, they wrote *legen*[24] on a piece of paper. "*Legen,* what is that?" I asked. They repeated *legen* in another place on the paper and underlined it. "Do you mean *Lægen,* the doctor?" "Yes, yes, yes," they nodded. "I have no use for any doctor," I said. "I'm not sick."

The doctor was on the second floor and I scrambled upstairs. In my excited state I said all sorts of things; jabbering on, I complained that I was exhausted, that I ought to have been allowed to come by boat. The stenographer took it down, the doctor was patient and wanted to help me. "If you didn't come by boat it must be because the train is so much faster," he said. "Sure, only five hours *slower*," I said.

I asked what his name was. "Ruud," he said. "I'm so tired, I have to sleep," I said.

*

A short preface.

So, checked in at the Psychiatric Clinic in Oslo, an institution for the "nervous and mentally ill." It is 1945, from October 15 and on. My days are spent writing answers to Professor Langfeldt's* written questions. These answers are rush jobs on my part, written under the most adverse circumstances, within the time strictly allotted by regulations, in much too poor light, in a state of increasing depression. So I don't mean to say they are a collection of gems. But they are *my* work.

Since there was no time to make a copy of my answers and the Professor has refused to lend me the originals, I have nothing I can insert in this gap.

---

*Professor Gabriel Langfeldt, Ph.D. in medicine, the Psychiatric Clinic.

*

It is 1946, February 11.

I'm no longer in the institution.

That is not to say that I'm free, but I can breathe again. To breathe is also really the only thing I can do for the time being. I'm extremely depressed. I've come from an institution for health and feel extremely depressed. I was well when I went there.

Perhaps there will be time later to come back to my stay in the Psychiatric Clinic: the friendly nurses, the sincerely kind head nurse, Christmas '45, the patients, my short walks out-of-doors—it will all have to wait. I must recover.

First, I must try to get permission to return to Landvik Old People's Home. It won't be easy; the home is under new management, my old room is occupied by another oldster, the house is full. Chief of police Onsrud in Arendal did what he could for me, and everyone in the home also showed his good will, so I got in.

And now my recovery was supposed to begin. But I was no youth, and it was hard for me to get back to my normal life, interrupted four months ago; my convalescence took one month after another. I refused to see anyone, letters came but I didn't answer, I just couldn't bother. I took my walks in the slush, but afterward I was trembling. I dozed and slept a lot, even when I sat on a chair in the middle of the day. The people here said it was due to fatigue.

I pulled myself together and managed to send the sheath knife away. Oh, that knife! I hadn't appropriated it, it had got stuck to me at Grimstad Hospital and then been buried for four months, together with the rest of my things, in the basement of the clinic. I sent it by mail to the hospital: "Here is a sheath knife, please take it away, I can't stand seeing it anymore, it's not mine."

In other ways, too, I tried to put my affairs in order as well as I could. I checked off important days on the calendar, took out subscriptions to a couple of papers without permission, and mended my clothes. It's full winter, but with sparkling sunshine and longer and longer days; it's a sort of equatorial time: at 7 twilight before nightfall, at the next 7 o'clock light breaking toward morning. It holds good very nicely for a while, until the equator shifts.

At this time I had no desire to read. I had, of course, the history of civilization, the Bible and the work on New Guinea, but I quickly tired of regular books and preferred to read trash and newspapers. Now and then, in the kitchen, I came upon some religious magazine or other that I would pore over; the things were well written and often well thought out. There was the magazine *The Evangelist*, which was sent here free of charge, and various Adventist publications provided by lay preachers. The paper and print of the latter publications were exquisite, they were a feast to leaf through and restful for my impaired vision. I couldn't help thinking of my friend from Kløttran in Nordland, he could have joined this vast Adventist organization and been largely spared from going barefoot. But he had to go alone, he said.

One evening the head nurse at Grimstad Hospital came over by car. Her errand was to give me back—the sheath knife!

I wasn't great shakes at thinking deep yet, and I just stood there.

"You know," she said, "this sheath knife that you sent me does not belong to the hospital, and we won't keep it. It's a handsome knife, but it's not ours."

"Not mine either," I said.

"You'll have to ask at home," she said, "it must have come from Nørholm."

I didn't ask, it was too much for me.

*

The days go by, the months go by, and I'm not getting much better. Some die in the home, we have plenty of old people to choose from here; some disappear but others take their places, and it has no effect upon those of us who remain, which is as it should be. The snow is gone and it's spring; I feel more and more like working, but I have no strength. I still do not answer letters.

Tobacco is not rationed anymore, but I take no pleasure in that either, not a bit. So what do I want, why am I so contrary? Spring and summer and all, but God, what a stupid state of affairs! I sharpen two fresh pencils with the sheath knife to be ready for a sublime explanation, but it refuses to come. So what shall I do? I'm turned upside down, that's the trouble; I'm fed up with myself, have no wishes, no interests, no joys. Four or five good senses dormant, and the sixth sense frittered away.

That I have to thank the Attorney General for.

*

Landvik Old People's Home, Grimstad, July 23, 1946
My dear Mr. Attorney General
Oslo

I have been in doubt whether to write this letter. It probably won't do me any good. Also, I should have other things to do, old as I am. My excuse is that I do not write for the present day, I write for any individual who may get to read this after us. And I write for our grandchildren.

After a couple of moves in the course of last summer, I was committed on October 15 to the Psychiatric Clinic in Oslo. The reason for this committal is a riddle to more than myself. It is called, officially, an institution "for the nervous and mentally ill," but I was neither nervous nor mentally ill. I was an old man and I was deaf, but I was hale and hearty when I was torn out of my normal life and work and locked up. Some day, perhaps, the question will be raised as to the basis for the Attorney General's arbitrary and unwise conduct toward me. You could have called me in and spoken with me for a moment; you did not. You could have procured a doctor's certificate saying that I needed to be committed; you did not. The district doctor examined me for ten minutes—"just a physical," as he called it—mentioned perhaps a "rather high blood pressure," mentioned perhaps my cerebral hemorrhage. Should blood pressure require committal for a psychiatric examination? Should a cerebral hemorrhage that has not left the slightest mark on my mental capacity be sufficient reason for committal? People who have had a cerebral hemorrhage are not so few, arteriosclerosis is not a rare or unusual illness. I know a man who suffered a cerebral hemorrhage, yet he has no less than two doctorates. He claims that the hemorrhage has done him no harm.

I have to assume that my name was unknown to the honorable Attorney General. But you could have sought information where it was to be found. Someone would surely have been able to tell you that I was not entirely unknown in the realm of psychology, that over a very long career as a writer

I had created several hundred figures—created them internally and externally like living people, in every psychological state and nuance, in dream and action. You did not seek this information about me. You handed me over sight unseen, so to speak, to an institution and a professor who also were not informed. To be sure, he came equipped with his textbooks and his learned tomes which he has learned by heart and taken his examinations in, but it was something else than this which was under consideration here. Since the honorable Attorney General was uninformed, the Professor ought to have dismissed me on the spot. He ought perhaps to have hesitated before showing up with his expertise here, where the job to be done was completely beyond his scope.

Besides—what was the purpose of it all? Was it to have me declared insane and thus not responsible for my actions? Was that the favor which the honorable Attorney General wanted to show me? If so, you reckoned without me. Already on June 23, in magistrate's court, I had from the very first moment assumed responsibility for what I have done, and ever since I have maintained this view unstintedly. For I knew in my heart that if I could speak without any restriction, the wind would turn around to acquittal for me, or as close to acquittal as I would dare to go and the court accept. I knew I was innocent, deaf and innocent; I would have done very well in an examination by the public prosecutor just by telling most of the truth.

But this situation was confounded by the circumstance of my being locked up month after month—forcibly, against my will, and by coercion, with prohibitions, torture, inquisition. I realize that the institution can procure fine testimonials that say something else. Let it! We do not all of us have the same susceptibilities, whether for good or ill, and achievements come about in different ways. Some live, rest and work by fits and starts, they don't get anywhere by thinking something through. Should they get a nibble at heaven's grace, it goes posthaste for the moment, while at other times there is nothing doing. For my part, I would have rather ten times over sit shackled in an ordinary prison than be forced to live together with those more or less mentally ill people in the Psychiatric Clinic.

But that is where I got stuck.

A prisoner is not to be spared. The Professor asked questions and I answered them; I wrote and wrote because I was deaf, taking pains to answer everything. I sat in the miserable light of a misted globe high up in the ceiling during the darkest months of the year, noticing that my eyesight was gradually getting weaker, but I wrote so that the experts and the scientists should not come to grief because of me. Then the Professor demanded that I give an account of my "two marriages," as he put it. I refused—the first time so emphatically that I thought it would suffice. But it did not suffice. The Professor repeated his monstrous question in writing and orally two more times, each time putting the blame on "the authorities." I didn't answer a word. It wasn't myself I wanted to screen, I wanted to prevent an outrage.

But the Professor was not at a loss. He obtained permission from "the authorities" to transport my wife from Arendal to the clinic in Oslo for an examination. The result of this session can be read on pages 132ff. of the magnum opus sent to the jury.

A prisoner is still not to be spared. Not for anything!

When at a certain point I thought I could glimpse the end of the expertise, the Professor had me undergo something that he called the judicial investigation or test. It turned out to be nothing other than the preceding. It was in every respect exactly the same as what had been asked and answered for months. Even the tone was unchanged; nor was there a new angle or anything better calibrated, a difference that would show that now we were working in depth. Nothing. It simply dragged out the whole thing, dragged it out for weeks and months.

The last time I ventured to look for the end, I was asked to account for three letters of mine that had been transmitted to the Professor. The letters were 50—fifty—years old and didn't deal with anything wrong that I had done, but rather with the very bad treatment I had suffered at the time when the notorious Mossin[25] was in the police. Now I had to write and rewrite again, because I was deaf; it was of no interest to the living or the dead anymore, but the episode served to torture me still a bit more. I did get over it now as well, to be sure, but during the last few weeks I kept my end up only by drawing on my reserves. When a friend found me and got me out, I was like jelly.

And what had it all been good for? Law and justice, a big apparatus. The examining magistrate's appointment of two psychiatrists nominated in advance, transports under police escort back and forth across the land, publicity involving visits by foreigners who were to be shown the incarcerated animal, four months to put learned labels on every conceivable state of mind I might get into—and then, at last, the verdict: *I was not, nor had I been, insane, but I had permanently impaired mental faculties.*

Unfortunately, yes. And they had been severely impaired precisely by my stay at the Psychiatric Clinic.

There were two experts, but one of them kept—or was kept—almost completely out of it. I saw the head twice, each time for maybe a quarter of an hour; he gave the impression of being straightforward and without conceit, one could talk with him. He only made the unexpected mistake of throwing in my teeth a report of my visit with Hitler, where I was supposed to have expressed anti-Jewish sentiments. I have not to this day read this report, much less acknowledged it. The idea of me attacking the Jews! I have had too many good friends among them for that, and these friends have been fine friends to me. I kindly request him to look through my collected production to see whether he can find any attack on the Jews.

What I have written about and against the Professor, the other expert, has not, of course, not been intended to question his competence per se. For that I lack every qualification. No doubt, he knows his things; that is, he knows *his* things. I merely maintain that his things did not concern me. Neither the man nor his trade was anything for me.

My dear Mr. Attorney General! When you announced the experts' verdict on me, you supplied the public at the same time with a statement to the effect that you had dropped the legal proceedings against me and waived the indictment.

Excuse me, but here again you acted without me. It did not occur to you that I might be dissatisfied with this decision; you forgot that in magistrate's court and ever since I have assumed responsibility for what I did and was awaiting the sentence. Your impulsive intervention caused me to dangle between heaven and earth, and yet my case was not resolved. Half of it remained. You thought that this would be good enough, but it was not, and I think that some people will agree with me. I was until recently not just anybody in Norway and the world, and it did not suit me to live out the rest of my days in a sort of amnesty from you, without being held responsible for my actions.

But you, honorable Attorney General, struck the weapon out of my hand!

You will no doubt think you have remedied this now—afterward—by a summons calling me before the Superior Court. It doesn't remedy anything, I have been pushed out of my firm and clean posture. What has now become of your "dropping of legal proceedings" and your "waiving of the indictment"? You allow your lawyers and office clerks to be interviewed about my case from every successive point of view; you are using me as a guinea pig for your most peculiar judicial methods. You could have taken your cue from my position at the hearing, and little by little avoided having to take directives for your actions from journalists and the press. And finally, what are you going to do about my four-months torment in the clinic? Am I to have it free of charge from your hands? Am I to have it as *advance* punishment, in addition to the one to come?

If I had been left in peace, my intention was to plead not guilty in Superior Court. The idea is not as farfetched as you may think. I do retain a remnant of my "permanently impaired mental faculties," and I would have used it, first, to discuss a certain material, and then to invite the court to consider my case with justice and nothing but justice.

But I have abandoned this plan, I have lost my courage. Even if the result in court should be favorable, there would be nothing to prevent another half turn of the screw in public opinion. I would once again have become a guinea pig.

Respectfully yours

*

The summer is going by. I don't feel any great difference between the seasons, they do not follow one another by months; the time is timeless and the summer is lost to me.

But something has happened. I'm not writing a book, not even a diary, God help me; I leap across wide expanses as the crow flies and do not keep track of what is happening. But something trickles through to me from the outside world, of course. The former manageress of the home has left and a new one come instead. One of the two beauties in the office downstairs has abandoned us, but the other is still there. Our old home for the aged has become too dilapidated for us and we intend to build a new one.

It's no trifling matter. I can tell by looking at us old folks that we have got something serious to mumble about; we are to have a bath, laundry, infirmary, bakery, hen house, woodshed and rooms for twenty or thirty people, all under one roof. We have never heard of such luxuries before, and our imagination is stirred in a way we haven't experienced since our youth. Some of us try to defend our old home, we have by no means been badly off here, and besides—isn't it the whole point that we are here to die? Yes, of course. But we must try to get our hands on as much as we can till the last moment. Shouldn't we keep up with the times, shouldn't we get modernized for a new home? Let's just have it all—we can perfectly well get accustomed to new necessities as we are about to leave, and die with a cigarette in our mouths.

Of course we shall die. But not quite yet, as St. Augustin says.

*

I go out to buy shoelaces. They are much too long and reach three times around my leg, but it doesn't matter. I find the man who is building a house on the hill. It's a disgrace to the eye—he's building his new roof at an oblique angle straight through an older roof which will continue to stay in place. Could my sighting from the road have been as bad as all that? The man has done construction work in America, so he must know what he's doing. But I cannot bring myself to go and and find out which of us is wrong. That's what I would have done last year, before I fell into the hands of doctors.

I have long racked my brain over getting my galoshes repaired now that fall is approaching. They go back to the First World War but still have good soles; it's just that the right one is torn and won't stay on my foot. It has been bothering me for years, but now it's gone quite haywire, because I happened

83

to stumble in it and had to carry it home in my hand. It's getting to be a great nuisance. I sew it up with good strong wool thread, but it doesn't work, the stitches tear and make everything worse. So that's the end of that; but they have been good galoshes, I have walked in them in many lands, tears and all, and they went with me to Vienna and to Hitler on a famous occasion. Now I would throw them ever so far away if it weren't that my shoes needed those thick soles to walk on. One thing is linked to the other. And I have tied up the torn overshoe with one of the shoelaces.

*

One, two, three, four—that's how I sit scribbling and jotting down tiny scraps for myself. It won't come to anything, it's just an old habit. I leak gingerly words. I am a dripping tap: one, two, three, four—.

Isn't there a star called Mira?[26] I could have looked it up, but I have nothing to look it up in. It doesn't matter. Mira is a star that appears, shines a little while and is gone. That's its whole course of life. And mortal man, here I think of you. Of all

84

living things in the world you are born to almost nothing at all. You are neither good nor evil, you have come into being without a reasoned purpose. You come out of the fog and again return to the fog, that's how utterly imperfect you are. And mortal man, should you mount some rare steed, nothing makes that steed rare any longer. Ever so, the day's journey, slowly—.

Do you jump off and throw your hat on the ground for a pair of eyes, a pair of eyes that you meet? You lack the spirit for that.

Just now a new and hopeful generation is swirling out of the depths. It is so newly born and innocent, I read about it but know no name; no matter. They are all will-o'-the wisps: they come, shine for a moment, and are gone. Come and go, as I came and went.

*

I had once an uncle in Hamarøy, a confirmed bachelor, stingy and hot-tempered, very taciturn, a so-called quick head and a man of means. He was no shining light, but he had a house at the parsonage and was postmaster for the whole parish—there wasn't a post office at every tenth house in those days. My uncle was a remarkable fellow of a kind, he had managed to buy a large house and a storehouse going with it from among the buildings at the parsonage itself. How he had been able to do this I do not know, but the parson, whom he must perforce have had to deal with, was called Bent Fredrik Hansen and later went to Ørlandet.[27] After him, Fredrik Motzfeldt Raum Fladmark came to us in Hamarøy, and later he went to North Odal.[28] The last one was Christian Engebret Nicolaisen, who went I don't know where, because I left home and lost sight of him. But all along my uncle lived in his large house with the storehouse, purchased from the parsonage.

Besides the mail, he was also in charge of the public library, which, in fact, he saved from utter decline. He bought and sold a bit without a license, got books for sale from the south, and also ordered books for the library at his own discretion. He asked nobody's permission. His housekeeper was called Sissel; she may have been a good person, but she starved me for several years.

My uncle was not an old man in my time, yet his hands were getting paralyzed and he couldn't write.

I was eight years old when I moved in with him, and was trained to do all his writing for him. This came about through shameful discipline. He himself lay fully dressed in a so-called settle bed all day, getting more and more paralyzed.

All this is unimportant.

But one day, when I may have been about nine years old, a very tall, dark man came into the post office, a huge giant. I looked at him in astonishment. He handed me a letter and a four-pence piece for a stamp.

My uncle began talking with him. His name was Hans Paulsen Torpelvand, and he actually lived in the neighboring parish of Tysfjord, but used our post office because it was closer.

"You're on the road today?" my uncle says.

"Yes. With a little letter to my son in Kristiania."

"I have read about him," my uncle said.

"Hmm," the father said. "Well, I too have read about him, but I understand very little of it."

"That's how it is."

"And his mother had hoped he would come back educated as a clergyman. But he isn't likely to do that."

My uncle answered from his settle bed, "His education is better than any clergyman's."

I don't know where my uncle had that answer from, in all likelihood from newspapers and books he nosed around in. But who was that hopeful son in Kristiania? Paul Botten-Hansen, no less.[29] He was one of the best men of his time in Norway.

My father had also once a hopeful son.

And such hopefulness takes more than a little care and nurture. But let us not turn tragical in our disappointment. The whole thing isn't worth that much.

*

A little spruce stands at the bottom of the neglected garden next door. What business is it of mine? Therefore I scarcely look in its direction. It's obviously in a bad way and will surely die. It's so small and pretty, about three feet tall and straight as a candle, but a huge poplar overshadows it and brushes its top day and night with its foliage, not giving it a moment's peace. If it didn't stand in my way—but there is no other way—or if it weren't so helpless! But it's none of my concern. Since I have nothing to do with it, I simply take a quiet little walk on dark fall evenings and cut away leaves and branches so that it will have peace for the night. But many mornings there are new leaves and new branches, and I cannot reach high enough. I have picked out a crate to stand on, but there is light in all the windows and a dog gives warning. Why not go in full daylight and clear away the leaves and branches once and for all? Last year I could have done that. But then I was not here, committed.

It's all so idiotic.

I keep an eye out for the neighbor, say hello and tell him, "You should trim the poplar and save that little spruce over there!" He doesn't reply, he must have read in the paper that they have had to give me a psychiatric examination. "I feel sorry for that little spruce," I say. Then the man smiles wryly up at an open window in the house and leaves me.

In my idleness I while away the time for another few dark fall evenings by cutting back some leaves and branches, but I cannot reach up, and the wind sways the new leaves and the new branches. It's hopeless.

But one morning a man with an ax and saw is

trimming the poplar from top to bottom. It's none of my business, but he seems to have received an order; he also trims some other large leafy trees at the same time. That's his affair.

Had someone perhaps sat behind the window and heard my conversation with the neighbor a few days ago, and seen his twisted smile? I make a guess at his wife.

Well, anyway, we won't know until next spring whether the top of the little spruce is still alive. A long time to wait.

*

Someone is calling me, I can hear it—.

But it isn't true, sheer delusion. I want to be interesting to myself. It is a remissness on my part not to have turned this little knob before, for the benefit of the psychiatrists, then I would have had an elegant name for it. Here I sit, hale and hearty, fooling myself on purpose. It must be schizophrenia, at least.

That someone should call me is sheer mischief, but the fact that I think it up for my own benefit is a bit thick—I wouldn't have tolerated it from someone else. Nobody called me, I was just pretending.

Why do I do it? My thoughts fly far and wide. I do it as an exercise, I do it to try and get back into shape again after my depression in the Psychiatric Clinic. It has gotten a little better now, after several months, but it refuses to let go completely. I was too old when the experiment was foisted on me, it will take time to get over it. I can only trust in my peasant wits and my general good health.

Is, then, the idea that someone was calling me pulled out of thin air? It can be traced back to a couple of Professor Langfeldt's questions: Had I ever experienced anything strange, anything that could be called supernatural? In my innocence I began to reconstruct a very deep and beautiful childhood experience, but it came to nothing, and all my efforts were wasted on him; he understood nothing. "But haven't you *heard* anything?" he asked. I didn't answer. Couldn't be bothered.

It was no doubt the recollection of this session that turned into someone calling me. I cannot think of anything more profound to say about it.

But I have finally cleared up the this-worldly puzzle of the sheath knife. That's something, at least. It came to me as something sweet and unexpected. Ah, we slaves to necessity don't see very much, can't come up with any ideas, have few intuitions. I ought to have figured it out by myself, but I didn't.

When Stevenson[30] was writing on his South Sea island, he heard a divine voice within him. He didn't ask any questions, didn't consult any books, he was a genius in eruption, he had revelations. He was ill, but made himself well by writing in a divine madness. He read about mankind in the age of concrete and died of a stroke.

Oh yes, the sheath knife is mine, it was sent to me long ago by Erik Frydenlund,[31] postmaster in Aurdal. Too bad I didn't have this good knife when I was out cutting leaves and branches on those dark fall evenings.

But how had the sheath knife gotten secretly to me at Grimstad Hospital? A very simple story: Little Esben had come along after all, and he was all too eager to get his hands on that big, wonderful knife, so his mother could think of nothing better than to hide it on the bottom of the woodbox. Fine. But then of course she forgot to alert me when she went back home.

While I'm writing this thing about the sheath knife, I had better also mention something else: I've got a new pair of galoshes. They are dressing me up there at home, they must have added up their kroner and øre and clubbed together.

But I have no use for new galoshes, I have tied up the old ones with the thick soles and worn them for many months now. What else should I have used my much too long shoelaces for, if not to tie things up with? And happily they are suitable for this use; you can barely see the lashing.

I don't intend to start using the new galoshes.

*

If only the winter were over. Oh, for heaven's sake, if only the winter were over!

My eyesight is a little impaired. It feels strange to me not to see well, and at first I didn't believe it was true, I thought I had gotten a piece of dust in my eyes. I was wearing my excellent glasses, which I could see so well with a few months ago; were they no good anymore?

I took a cab at great expense to the eye doctor. "Now listen: I cannot see clearly, not read as before, not thread a needle, what sort of phenomenon is that? Is there something wrong with both my eyes at the same time?" To this I don't get much of an answer, he turns the knobs to white lines and red lines and to letters and numbers. "There seems to be something wrong with my left eye," I say to help him out. He doesn't answer. I feel annoyed and persist: "Sure, when I cover my left eye I can still read large clear letters. But if I do a counter test and cover my right eye, all I see is a big black spot." "Hmm," he says. That annoys me even more, and I insist there must be something wrong with my left eye! "I'll be glad to give you some prismatic lenses," he says at last. "Of course I'll have prismatic lenses," I say. "There's also something called prismatic binoculars, and with them we see awfully well." "I don't think we should do anything more," he says, bowing.

Can you beat that! I ride home again furious with the eye doctor; I don't trust him, don't trust him one bit.

Now I find a way of getting to Oslo. Christmas is approaching, I have to hurry. Since I cannot sit straight up and down for twelve hours going by

94

train, I jot down the exact date when I can take the boat, and I'm off. It goes very smoothly, everyone is helpful; what's more, I am in high spirits on board, a man in his prime. Everything has been taken care of for me; I am in Oslo, walk to my hotel, get a meal and a shave and go to the eye doctor.

Here it starts becoming a bit stressful. It's a dreary day; it's raining, the streets are ghastly, and I can't see. I walk up four floors in some house and then down again. I suspect I've made a mistake and stand studying the numbers. Suddenly a gentleman says hello in front of me, he is with a young lady. "Can I help you with something?" he asks. "No, thanks, I'm just looking for an eye doctor," I answer. "There!" he says, pointing. The lady smiles. "How can you be bothered with giving directions to a stranger in this awful weather?" I ask. The lady smiles even more. "I recognized you," he says. I thank him with a deep bow and enter the building. Wasn't it here I was all the way up on the fourth floor once before? Now I comb every single floor and all the names and find the doctor. There are three ahead of me in the waiting room.

By force of habit I like to take a look at the newspapers and magazines, but I can't make out very much. I have to wait. The patients go out and come back in again by turns; a nurse comes to cheer me up, saying I will have to wait, but it won't be very long.

And now I have become quite calm, soon I expect to have my eyesight back again. How awfully friendly of that gentleman and lady to take the time to help me out in the rain. A patient speaks to me, but I'm deaf and have to nod at random. She goes on talking, and I point to my ears to indicate that my hearing has been terrible of late, but there is hardly anything wrong with my eyesight, only a bit of dust in my left eye. I'm in high spirits and chatter away. In the end the lady must have become suspicious of my various senses, so she let me be. I'm not called in for a long time. And now the lady has scribbled some words on a sheet of paper and shows it to me; she's thanking me for a couple of books or something of the sort—.

Once with the doctor, I'm made to try this, that and the other, but he is kind and doesn't subject me to red lines and letters. We try out eyeglasses and magnifying glasses, until I have to return to the waiting room again. Now it was the lady's turn to go in, and I didn't see any more of her.

The rest of the visit went quickly. The doctor suggested to me that I dictate. "Dictate? I can't, I never could." But why should I dictate? After all, I don't write any more, I stopped doing that many years ago. However, it might be nice to have my eyesight back again and be able to read a little and such. "Ye-es, of course." He called the optician and arranged something for the month of January, I had to wait. "But can't you let me have some glasses right now?" I asked. "Let me see your glasses. These should be good glasses," he said. "Oh, capital," I said; "up to a few months ago I could see just as clearly with them as I did in my youth, but now I probably need different glasses, a little stronger perhaps, or what?" He wrote out a prescription—I scarcely looked at it, but it was to be filled in January. No, I got no glasses, but instead something curious that I hadn't asked for: a prescription for a hand-held magnifying glass and a bottle of iodine! I could drop by the pharmacy and pick up the iodine right away, he said. When I wanted to pay him, he waved me away with his hand and turned back to his desk.

97

And so I came back to the hotel with a bottle of iodine and a prescription for a magnifying glass which was to be had at the optician's in January. For my eyesight I got nothing.

A queer sort, these eye doctors. I have received a poor impression of them.

But otherwise my stay in Oslo was sheer pleasure and joy, the most delightful Christmas I have ever experienced in a hotel. I took walks all around, visited my children and grandchildren, went to exhibits, and padded cheerily about looking at the city of Oslo after umpteen years. Many things were new to me, the bus traffic, all the restaurants, a completely unfamiliar young generation bustling about night and day. All were helpful and courteous on my walks, offering to give me their seats or their newspapers, and to open the door for me when they saw I was getting off; but I had been a streetcar conductor in Chicago and managed by myself. All in all I couldn't perceive any cooling-off in their friendliness toward me, though I was still in custody. A young lady stopped me in the middle of Karl Johan Street, said something, laughed, and threw her arms around my neck. I remember she had brown eyes. A gentleman with a rucksack on his back looked at me and said, "You don't wear galoshes in this weather? Come with me and we'll get you some." He pulled at me and tried to take me with him. When he became a nuisance I thanked him and escaped into the hotel.

But there was a lot of trouble with the boats over the holidays; I had to wait for some that never showed up and for others that had their runs canceled. It took me ten days to get back to the old people's home.

*

My affairs are in a disgraceful mess; I haven't answered letters, or thanked for flowers and small gifts with cards and greetings. It's now the second year that I have neglected to thank my good publisher in Barcelona, he never forgets to send a wire wishing me a happy new year. There is a pile of letters from abroad at the bottom of my suitcase, and many more from last year. They don't know that I am in jail, they cannot imagine that I haven't received a post after the "changeover." But I can.

The days are going by.

I still do not understand much of what is happening in the world; I read the papers and study the dispatches, but I fall short, I must recover more. The trip to Oslo was good for me, even if I got no remedy for my eyes. We tether a domestic animal mildly, giving it a wide latitude, and leave it alone. All right, it's tethered. Still, I must be grateful for the official mildness that allowed me to make the trip, it would have been worse if it hadn't come off. After all, many things happened. I didn't exactly look like a fine specimen of an old man to the lady who embraced me on Karl Johan. No. And I was not ragged but had on a handsome coat for the gentleman who wanted to give me galoshes. And besides those two, ever so many others showed me friendliness. I'm neither hated nor despised by people. And that's good. But if I were, it wouldn't have mattered to me. I'm so old.

*

One of the things I find it difficult to understand is why those who write for the papers are keeping up their own and the public's interest in my "case," and why this case continues to be postponed.

Last summer it was postponed no fewer than three times at different points. And it changed nothing that on May 1, '46, I received a solemn summons to appear in Superior Court, solemnly served upon me by the Grimstad Police. It changed nothing. The case was only—postponed till the fall, September! Anyway, it was quite a jump. But beg pardon, next the case was postponed from September '46 to March '47. It was getting to be a farce with tightrope tricks. I won't take note of anything further.

Had I not perhaps taken pains to stay on top of things and keep informed? But I saw nothing but unrest and changes of tenure wherever I turned. First, the Attorney General retired. Then the regular judge in my district quit and took over his old office as chief magistrate of the county. Then one day our district attorney left us to become a judge in the neighboring county. I was informed time and again that my case was *complete*. It just never got to court.

I ponder and try to find out whether there may be some judicial advantage to these "postponements." Could it be possible that somebody is gambling on my old age and hoping that I'll die, die of myself? But if so, my case would be for ever undecided, so what would be the advantage? Wouldn't it be every bit as smart to do something about me while I am still alive? Besides, waiting for someone to die must be one of the most boring and never-ending things imaginable. Certain heirs would have a word to say in that connection.

Boganis[32] tells about a dog that had been thrown off the scent but picked it up again as it plunged across a ditch—and so it simply continued on the other side. He sure did, he simply continued.

More things that continue: My latest postponement was until March '47, right? It's now March '47, or it's April, as a matter of fact. But today I read that I have been postponed "until sometime in the summer." I don't make any fuss about it, just nod to show I'm familiar with the phenomenon. After '47 comes '48. A domestic animal is tethered.

It may very well be that from now on it is more practical to postpone me by half a year and a year at a time. For how else will they get the better of my tenacious hold on life through all those future years of mine? Imagine being thwarted by such a bad joke!

Now the Supreme Court is being blamed, for not being able to finish its work on my case. It's nice to have something solid as a rock to blame.

*

Isn't it a fact that a long, long time ago there was more joy in being alive for us human beings than today? Maybe I'm quite aware that this is the wrong question to ask and that it is poorly written, but I do it on purpose. It touches something in me, whatever it may be, perhaps a sufferance of my own shortcomings. An intentional helplessness, an infection from the Bible.

A word by Bunyan occurs to me: "As I walked through the wilderness of this world, I lighted on a certain place—."[33] Here ends my recollection of Bunyan. But I was left with a sweet sufferance of the expression. A stroke of luck of imperfection.

A Lapp who came from the mountain plateau and got to see green fields and forests, made a *joik*[34] about it and said, "It's so beautiful I have to laugh!" It was said in song, but it was more than song. "Selah!" David says. I do not know what "selah" means,[35] but David says it. It's beautiful.

God bless everything that is not just ordinary human speech which we have to understand. Silence also has God's blessing.

During the war I could sometimes tell by the looks of others that now there was shooting going on. But I couldn't hear any cannons, perhaps because it was too far away. My deafness was an advantage, but only as long as it was not a question of pistols or gunshots; then my deafness, quite frankly, was a lousy help. I can still hear brief cracks, even faint taps on the door with a knuckle, but I'm deaf and can't hear or understand the flow of human speech. It just sounds like a continuous buzzing. Nobody has spoken to me for such a long time that I have myself forgotten how to speak; I've been alone, have seen well until recently but not heard. I have approached the position of certain Orientals: the necessary silence. I don't even talk to myself anymore, for lack of bad habits.

But I can no longer see as I used to, that's worse than the deafness. To be sure, I was supposed to get a magnifying glass in January, but though it's now spring, I do not yet have it.

But at least it's spring, thank God!

I walk by the little spruce which stands there in the snow, alive. I walk by and do not stop even for a moment in front of the windows, and I say to myself, Well, no, you can't tell anything about that spruce for a long time yet, so just walk past! But of course, already in March everybody could see that the top was alive.

In thirty years it will be a tall spruce, timber.

There is such a dearth of songbirds around here. It has been a severe winter and many must have died, only a lean crow or magpie flaps its wings now and then near the buildings of the old people's home. One day I thought I had caught sight of a belated harbinger of spring, but since I didn't see well enough I couldn't decide whether it was a starling, or a blackbird that had wintered. At all events it had risked its life in this place, there are four huge cats around.

*

When I take my daily walks in the slush I sometimes run into a little yellow dog who doesn't mind being talked to and petted, otherwise I never see a soul along the whole way. It suits me fine to be all by myself and not have to ask twice what people are saying to me. And little by little the snow melts off the guard stones so I can recognize them from previous walks, the sun has become nice and warm, and already many a small forest path begins to appear. I think of Martin from Kløttran in Hamarøy, it's now a year or a year and a half since he came to me here in the woods. He too had to go it alone, but he had a mission, I do not. He walked about in the land praying to God.

A branch stirs, there is a small bird on it. I stop short. Sitting on a branch of another tree is another small bird; they seem to belong together, a pair of sparrows that flew toward each other and met and separated five times right to my face. It takes place in the air—they quiver together for a second and part and meet again, five times. Afterward they look as if they hadn't done it. The male was particularly audacious and seemed inclined to put the whole blame on her. I didn't raise an outcry, no, I didn't, but I let him know in righteous indignation that he was a low and unchivalrous soul—one had been as much to blame as the other. Shortly afterward the female made off, and serve him right, too!

I have no idea what St. Francis would say about this.

Ah, the infinitely small amid the infinitely big in this wonderful world! I'm glad to be alive again. The trip to Oslo did me good.

*

What is the feeling of spring, this sense of burgeoning which every year plays havoc with our psyche? God only knows. A female missionary in a foreign land would probably call it the voice from her homeland, in order to give a religious and otherworldly tinge to it; I, on the other hand, discover it for myself and mean it literally: it does have something to do with home and homeland. We want to be back again, we want to go home. We have no feeling of spring abroad, but merely feel a nod inside us for a new place. A nod without a heart.

A memory of 1898 or '99 from Helsingfors.[36] But it is nearly fifty years old and not reliable anymore; I have forgotten some names and the sequence may have shifted.

There were two in the bookstore when I came in: one was a bareheaded middle-aged fellow in tall jackboots and with a white shirt outside his trousers, the other a younger man with a trowel in his hand. There was nobody behind the counter.

"Coming right away," said the first one to me. "The girl is only upstairs to get a book for me."

I found a chair and sat down.

"I'm a Russian," the man said.

"Imagine boasting about something like that!" mocked the man with the trowel.

"I'm from Norway," I said.

The Russian, interested: "Really, from Norway. Do you intend to stay here?"

"Yes, for a year."

"It doesn't matter what country we're from," the mason said. "I'm from Finland, from the world." His words fell on deaf ears.

The Russian came up to me: "I haven't seen you before, where do you live in town?"

"I don't live in town, I live far out, on Føllisø Road."

"I have to live here in town and wait, but I don't like it here."

The Russian talked freely. He had been with his master and mistress, who had gone, he didn't know where, disappeared to some faraway land. But he was tired of waiting, didn't like it here and wanted to go home. How come he spoke Swedish when he was a Russian? Well, he had learned it as a child and all through the years afterward, his parents were Swedish Finns. They were dead, but he himself was born in Russia and was a Russian.

"That you aren't ashamed," the mason said. But nobody listened to him.

I thought to myself that this must mean the Russian was born in captivity in some remote northern province, but I didn't understand how he could now be here, and I didn't feel like asking him.

He went on talking, saying he had a cottage, a nice red-painted cottage, with many trees and a forest and a little brook flowing past. Oh, good God! And his wife and children were waiting for him; he himself worked for the lord of the estate, oh, a very big estate, miles and miles, hundreds of servants and workers.

The young lady came down from the second floor with a book for him. The man threw himself on it, crossed himself and put it in his pocket. "I'm expecting some money," he said to the woman, "lots of money, I'll pay you very soon. This gentleman is from Norway," he said about me.

The woman smiled.

"He's going to be here for a year, but I don't like it here and want to go home."

The woman looked at me: "May I help you?"

"I'd like a small Russian-Swedish dictionary."

The Russian took his book from his pocket again, crossed himself and turned the pages. On the cover there was some icon or other.

"What sort of book is that?" asked the mason. He didn't receive an answer and went on: "A saint's legend. I would put it on my trowel and toss it far away."

"But it's dear to him," said the woman behind the counter.

The mason turned to me: "What can one say to such lunacy? They are like animals, know nothing, read saints' legends, cross themselves. 'I was born in Russia and am a Russian,' he says. Isn't that a matter of indifference?"

"No, no," the woman said.

"What do you mean, miss?" the mason asked in a raspy voice.

"It's not a matter of indifference. We do have a land, our motherland."

"Exactly! That's the sort of talk we're born and brought up with, we read it in the papers and hear it in the marketplace. But would you like to know what I think?"

Suddenly the Russian exclaims in ecstasy, "Oh, my great, holy Russia!"

"His homesickness has made him hysterical," the woman said to me.

The mason gets ready to leave us, to leave the whole place, in fact; his face is pale and he says angrily, "The motherland—oh, go away! What nonsense! Do you want to know what I think? About the motherland, with love and falling on one's knees, and all the rest of the sticky stuff. Yeah, would you like to hear what I think? The motherland is wherever we are doing well. Yes, that's what I think. The motherland is just that and nothing else."

The saleslady smiles at him: "That's the sort of thing you are teaching the other masons, isn't it?"

He is taken aback. "What do you know about that?"

"I've heard about it. You speak at the union meetings."

A moment after the mason had left, two men came in, travelers speaking English; they asked for a map of Finland.

The Russian introduced himself: "I'm Russian."

"Hssh," the woman said softly.

The two men talked together at the counter. They also wanted a big map of Russia to see where they had been. "We've come from China," they explained, "an endless journey, for months on end, through all of Russia. We are Americans."

The woman spoke English and could answer them.

"What are those gentlemen saying?" asked the Russian.

"Hssh," the woman said.

"I would only like to know if they've come from Russia."

"Yes, they've come from Russia."

"Oh, Jesus Christ be praised, then they've come by the great railroad that has no end." He mentioned by name provinces and many cities, he mentioned a yellow station house at the estate, and twenty versts from there was his home. He crossed himself. Beg pardon, but they must have passed the big yellow station house, there was no mistaking it, and his cottage was only another twenty short versts further on. It sat by the brook among the poplars and the juniper bushes, and the small birds were too numerous to count.

"What does that man want?" the Americans asked.

The woman smiled. "He wants to know if you rode past his house in Russia."

The Americans, confused: "What? We don't know. His house in Russia?"

"He's so plagued by homesickness. His master and mistress have gone away, and he's been left behind here—"

"He has been abandoned here?"

"He was ordered to go home at once and given money for the journey. But he went to the bad and drank up the money."

"Poor fellow!" the Americans said, laughing. "And now he longs to go home? So do we," they said. "It's a sickness, we're quite familiar with it. Anyway, we're taking the boat home straightaway."

"I wish you a pleasant voyage."

"Thank you. Where did you learn to speak English?"

"In America. I'm just home for a visit."

"Is that so!" nodded the Americans. "You'll be back with us, then?"

"That's the idea."

The Russian once again: "Ask them if they saw the small birds, at least."

"I can't ask about that," the saleslady said, kindly.

The Americans said goodbye and left. At the door they turned around and asked the saleslady if it would help any if the man got money for the trip home.

"I don't think so," she answered. "He probably has to wait for new orders from his master."

"Now they're gone, and I didn't find out!" the Russian sniffled. "Beg pardon, but they're bound to be there when I get home, don't you think?"

"Who? The sparrows? Sure, they'll be there."

"You should've seen them, miss, they would fly down to the brook and stick their beaks into it, just as if they were thirsty too, the wee little things!" The Russian wept. "Some miserable birds they were," he said, pulling himself together, "gray and yellow, and no sooner chased away than they came back again, the sky was black with them, a million—."

The tears trickled down into his gray beard.

I got tired of his hysteria and couldn't help wondering about the woman's patience with him.

She answered, "I'm a Finn and homesick myself!" And she bent forward and whispered over the counter to me, "I'm his cousin, I gather. But I won't let him know that."

*

One wet, foggy day I was wandering about downtown. It was between the wars and I was idle at the time. I was carrying some books I had bought, a couple of parcels a bit awkward to carry because they refused to stay in place and kept slipping out of my hands. I was actually on my way to the post office with a book for the Red Cross.

Then something happened.

A young man suddenly popped up, called me by name and said, "I'll have to hit you!"

He was well dressed and didn't look like a thief. "Yes, I'll have to hit you," he said again, seeming embarrassed and catching his breath. I stopped, and so did he. "No, that was a stupid thing to say, a stupid beginning, but I was wondering if I could hit you for some help—"

"I thought you were going to let fly at me."

"Oh no, far from it. I'm having some trouble, it makes me terribly unhappy to have to ask you, but I wanted to know if it would get me anywhere."

"Some help?"

"Yes, some help. I usually don't do such things, but I'm so hard up."

I gave him my book parcels to hold and reached into my pocket; at that time I had a few pennies to spare. As I was getting ready some money, I thought in my haste that it wasn't a miserable small bill he was asking for, but a help. By the way, he had an honest and attractive face.

While I was fiddling with this, he began to walk slowly. I didn't pay attention until he had moved on several steps; I said, "Here you are!" and followed him. But by now he had gotten a good way ahead, and I called to him and held out my hand with the money. He walked on. I called a few more times, but he increased his speed and was already far up Pilestrædet Lane. He disappeared into a side street.

I was all agape. Now I have experienced this too! I had to let out a fatuous, surprised laugh standing there.

And so the young man had made off with my book parcels, that was clear. But if he had figured on my books being worth more than my handout, he had figured wrong. I made good money by his faulty speculation.

But this was not what occupied me then. I was interested in figuring him out a bit more closely.

Why did he begin by wanting to "hit" me? To steel himself, to give himself courage in case he was turned down. Anyway, he quickly abandoned this tactic and collapsed. The next thing was that he felt embarrassed to be trusted with my book parcels—he who had come asking for help! If I had looked up I would have noticed the embarrassment in his face and made him even more embarrassed, but I was busy. He was in an awkward position and shifted his feet, moving one foot forward. Originally he didn't have the faintest idea he wanted to give me the slip, not at all; he tried to put up a bold front, feeling it bucked him up, but his one step pulled others after it, until he took to walking and seeking cover.

But he felt anything but comfortable, he had gotten himself into an odious scrape. He had heard my cries and could have turned back in time, but to turn around and confront me *after this* would be the worst of all, so what in the world was he to do?

Young man, evidently you aren't used to being in want, you have no practice in asking for help. You gave the impression of being of good family and of being yourself an upright young man. A "momentary difficulty" had swelled to such proportions that you thought you needed a "help," maybe a milk bill or some other trifle. Good heavens, you will encounter far worse things in life.

As for the books, there they lie in front of you; you cannot have them sent back to the owner, nor can you have them lying there on the table in plain sight of everybody. Won't you do your best to get rid of them, sell them? I ask because it is a way out. You flinch from turning them into money, since they aren't your books, after all; your hesitation does you honor. But can you afford it? Pardon me for meddling, but you will take the books to Omtvedt's. They are new, bound copies, you will get enough to pay the milk bill.

How did you happen to burn your fingers with these books anyway? It can all be explained. You probably wanted to spare an old man from fumbling with bills in the street and attracting attention. That was a nice thought. Obviously you also knew in your heart of hearts that I couldn't overtake or pursue you. And you really couldn't call out "Stop thief!" yourself, could you? In the end you had got yourself into such a pickle that you may have thought of suicide. It can all be explained, of course.

But as for me, I don't dare stand here any longer; people are beginning to stare at me, I'll have to give you up, and besides I'm going to the post office—.

I sank into the ground!

The post office—the book for the Red Cross—Mrs. Vogt—.

Mrs. Ida Vogt had something to do with a raffle for the Red Cross and asked me for a book by myself for the lottery. I bought the book and wrote some words of wisdom in it. But it made only a poor gift, so I put a hundred-krone bill inside the book to make it more of a prize to raffle off. I had it nicely wrapped and was on my way to the post office with it.

But now everything had turned out differently.

A young man with an honest and attractive face must have stood in the bookstore and seen what was going on; dogging my footsteps, he waylaid me and twirled me around his little finger.

He went home with the book. He sure did.

As for Mrs. Vogt, I had to send her another copy with fresh words of wisdom. And I received a wonderful thank-you note from the lady for my hitting on the idea of the hundred-krone bill.

*

I believe I promised at some earlier point that I might get back to my time at the Psychiatric Clinic. True, I didn't promise very much, but I shouldn't have promised anything at all or even mentioned it. To this very day I am reminded of what my stay there destroyed for me. It cannot be measured, it has nothing to do with weights and measures. It was a slow, slow tearing up by the roots.

What was to blame? Nobody in particular, nothing in particular, a system. Lording it over living life, regulations without intuition and heart, a psychology of squares and rubrics, an entire science founded on spite.

Others can endure the torture, that doesn't concern me, I could not. Something the psychiatrist ought perhaps to have understood. I was a healthy person, I turned into jelly.

I'm not in the habit of complaining and being dissatisfied with the world and with life, nor am I here. I'm no sourpuss; I joke a lot, laugh easily, have a sunny disposition. In this I take after my father, who was known for the same things. For other good traits I may have, I owe thanks to my mother. I'm a product.

But I'm not writing my life.

I'm now going to jot down a few random events, unimportant recollections from the men's wing of the Psychiatric Clinic. I shall add a couple of serious matters that will come up on their own, though I bring them back to mind again with great distaste.

It is an institution organized and managed along rather jesuitical lines, with half a dozen full-grown men to help out just in case, and with a myriad of white nurses who brighten up the place by swooping down on the rooms like a roar of white pigeons. They were kind sisters, and the male nurses were able. In the basement was a workshop for patients who were to have physical exercises, and on an upper floor was the laboratory where the proper person was to conduct his experiments and make his discoveries in the field of psychology. In between were the living units allocated to a half hundred "nervous and mentally ill" persons. The time was at sixty minutes to the hour because it was impossible to be more precise. There was order and punctuality everywhere, there was coldness, impersonality and regulations everywhere; there was discipline and religion.

I learned by experience that regular and mental hospitals are very different things, though both are institutions for health care. I acquired some familiarity with mental hospitals, but at night I lay wishing I were instead in an ordinary hospital, an ordinary prison, doing ordinary guard duty or hard labor, anything but being confined to the psychiatric loony bin at Vindern.[37] I lived there for four months, I shouldn't have been there even for a day. I wasn't a patient, after all, I was a lodger, a boarder.

I began in the first ward, in a cell with a peephole in the door; I was given a spoon to eat my food with. I mustn't cough too loudly, I mustn't open a parcel of underwear from home myself, and I mustn't be allowed to keep the string. After spending a couple of months there, I moved up one floor. Here I didn't get a cell but a small room with an ordinary door that could be closed, for which I was grateful. It was lighter and friendlier, not quite so insane, I got a knife and fork to eat with and, after a while, my watch. But there was the same frisking, the same atmosphere of secret snooping. My papers and books were thumbed through on the pretext of putting them in order, and for a long time I had to put up with having my clothes taken from me at night and hung somewhere else.

I saw no difference worth mentioning between the patients up here and on the first floor; perhaps a few more who received shock treatment and were supposed to rest afterward. We mixed with one another on our airings, except that I who couldn't hear had to keep to myself so I wouldn't trouble others to talk to me, or myself to repeat my questions all the time.

One day a tall, dark beauty stopped and smiled in my direction. She was dressed as a nurse under her dark coat; I hadn't seen her before, but I got up from my bench, nodded to her and said that I didn't hear. "Oh, I know that!" I could see she answered. Then she strolled off.

For a few weeks I didn't see her. But one Sunday—I think it was a Sunday—she emerged from the women's wing dressed for traveling; she was carrying a small bag and was with some man. I bowed to her and stood still. She came straight up to me and said she would like to shake hands with me and thank me for some of my books. I asked her if she was going away, but she replied that she was just taking a walk with her husband. She was very friendly and took pains to talk close to my ear. Later, I saw her now and then in the strolling areas—no, she was hardly a nurse, I had been mistaken, she was a patient, nervous, over-excited, a lady.

Another Sunday—if it was a Sunday—a young man greeted me; he was walking with an elderly lady who may have been his mother. He didn't say anything, only nodded. The lady took no part in it, but turned away. After a week he came again, repeating his greeting, and after another week he repeated it again, and the lady turned away each time. He may have acted against her will, so I wanted to prevent her getting even more annoyed; I bowed to him and remarked that perhaps he didn't know I was in custody, that I had been remanded here by the police. I didn't hear his answer, but I picked up the words: "Just as precious to me!" Afterward I saw neither him nor the lady anymore.

It was something of a riddle to me how the service personnel were able to endure this place. The men incurred little risk, but the nurses would sometimes start at a fairly early age and stay around for twenty years. Might I ask what sort of salary they received? No answer. Pension? No answer. Time off? Well, yes, certain days! Then I didn't feel right about asking any more questions.

But here the riddle began for me. Many of the nurses were kind, with good manners and cultivated speech, they were educated women; they had schooling, had read books before they started, but read no more. Could they really stand not being able to read anymore? Oh yes, easily. Of course, there were Sunday papers and Holy Scriptures and religious books lying around everywhere, but as far as I could see none of the nurses showed any interest in them. Officially the place was religious, but that didn't prevent their being human on the side as far as possible—and many things were possible. If a nurse did something wrong, it wouldn't be bruited about. In all other situations in life she would call witnesses if necessary; that was not necessary here, she was protected by her own and everyone else's silence, that was the system. If she meets up with something that she has to answer for, she doesn't answer. If appearances are against her, she will simply *put up with* having appearances against her. Not everyone can do that, but she can. She can summon a male nurse to witness her putting up with it. When a nurse has served for a long time, she will have learned enough practical Jesuitism to last her for life. And in death she needs nothing but a parson with the forgiveness of sins.

I often recall those kind nurses. I feel sorry for them. The place is very stuffy, and there they walk around growing old. No comfort, no cheer, never any laughter, God forbid they should laugh. Many were so nice, I could give names but don't dare to for fear it might harm them. In their cradles they had heard songs about love, children and home. Now they were hearing songs about three locked doors to life. And time goes by. Then they no longer think of anything, they are simply there.

As I was struggling through my days there, nothing occupied my mind more than the wish that my stay in the clinic would come to an end. I felt more and more tortured, more and more hollowed out; nothing reconciled me to my role as a guinea pig for the science of psychiatry, and nothing of a personal nature brought me close to the administration. We passed one another on the stairs and in the hallways without opening our mouths.

At the top was Mr. Langfeldt, medical director of the institution and professor at the university. I had never heard his lectures, nor would I, as a man in the street, have been qualified to entertain an opinion about them. I suspect that not all of his students are equally delighted with his teaching, something that applies to teachers in several disciplines. I go by my personal impression and intuition, by both alike; I go by episodes, facts, and whatever psychological sense I may possess. I hinted at my attitude to Professor Langfeldt in my letter to the Attorney General, and it has undergone no change since then. He strikes me as a typical college graduate, one who has come back from college with all the book learning he has picked up from schoolbooks and learned tomes, and which he has of course brought up to date through later studies. Obviously, I know nothing about the latter, I simply include it and presuppose it; I certainly do not need it.

He is so secure in his knowledge. But that is not the same as being secure in the old wisdom: nothing can be known for certain! In his personality and manner, Mr. Langfeldt stands there high and mighty, with his incontrovertible learning, his silence vis-à-vis objections, in general with his commonplace superiority that seems to be mere affectation.

During one of his rounds I observed the female assistant physician giving him an explanation several minutes long, stopping the entire procession while he quietly listened. Whereupon, without a word to the woman, or even a nod, he went on, followed by his staff. The same assistant physician happened on one occasion to laugh aloud at a story, a joke—he just *looked* at her.

I would wish the psychiatrist had the ability to

bring a smile to his lips. A smile that on occasion might also apply to himself.

His cool and dignified manner is hardly quite genuine, but rather assumed for the sake of the place and the surroundings. He is not an ossified or hardened man, for then he wouldn't be so well organized and so active. Besides fulfilling his responsibility as a teacher and a scientist, he finds time to write medical guides with household remedies for the country's families, even occasionally to provide a biological article for the subscribers to the popular monthly *Samtiden.*[38] He is young in years, with good publicity, and is no doubt a member of any number of learned societies. No, he is not hardened. Others may be, but he's not. His rigidity is due to affectation. He has enough verve both to remain dead silent and to speak his mind.

I shall mention at random a few examples of the latter.

The servants had damaged my shaving kit by cutting up the leather of the strop and, what's more, throwing away an important part of the whole equipment. It couldn't be found anywhere. Whereupon the servants went their way, leaving me in the lurch. A nurse who had been in service for twenty years took me into a cubicle and let me start shaving myself, without a mirror and with her razor or somebody else's, and I cut myself badly. Suddenly we heard a roar, it was the Professor. A regular roar: We had chosen the wrong place for my shaving, he snorted, making slips of the tongue, saying "young girl" (40–50 years old), before checking himself; he stood there a long time and stared, without moving on, oh no, he was rallying! It was some sight. The nurse was paralyzed, I wiped away soap and blood. Uttering a sound of protest was out of the question; she could have defended herself with a few words, mentioning the servants—it wasn't an option before the Professor, impossible.

I'm not entirely unaccustomed to having people work for me, and I wonder how I would have fared if I had let out an angry roar to a worker in such a situation. I think that, instead of roaring, I would have gone my way without letting on.

One morning the Professor came right up to me and said, "I think you must be mistaken. You were wearing glasses when you were in Hardanger,[39] too!" This was probably his way of showing his staff how infinitely deep his investigation of me went, almost back to the womb. But I was just as infinitely tired of his chatter about my glasses, which had no psychological significance whatever. I was in Hardanger in 1879, nearly seventy years ago, in the first flush of youth, that is. I could easily have given him a complete explanation, but I didn't bother. One day the doctor came to the farm where I stayed; it was raining, and he was wearing a black rain cape and a black rain hat. He had a hyphenated name, Maartman-Hansen or something. Since the nearest pharmacist and optician were in Bergen—an endless day's journey away—the doctor had brought with him, in a suitcase, the medicines and glasses which were most in demand. That was how I got my glasses in Hardanger!

But of course, he had to demonstrate his psychological expertise to the staff!

I was summoned to the Professor. The one who brought the summons kept shifting his feet to get me quickly on my way. I found the Professor and his staff in the office. I was presented with the three letters I have mentioned in my statement of July 23, '46 to the Attorney General, about which I had already said all I wanted to say. I must have made a gesture of impatience, for suddenly the Professor said, annoyed, "Don't lose your temper now, nobody's going to do you any harm!" This was said, not to one of the young disciples sitting below his lectern, but to an old man. And how casually he expressed himself: Nobody, he said, was going to do me any harm, while in reality he could answer only for himself. I made that very objection. Vexed, the Professor rose to his feet. Without introduction, without orienting his staff, he asked me loudly, "Did you ever borrow money from women?" (It said so in the anonymous letters.) I must have gaped at him, I must have stammered. On a previous occasion I had had to remind the Professor that we were not alone, but now I did not do so; I don't think I got around to saying anything, I just mumbled. I'm not aware of ever having borrowed money from women, but if I did I probably repaid the loan. But why bring up this question here? In the big dossier for the court, the Professor has tried to smooth over this episode in writing. I don't recognize it anymore.

But that was the tone. He wanted to show off to his staff. That was how Professor Langfeldt would allow himself to speak to a blameless old man. He knew that the staff would remain silent. The staff consisted of four doctors and many nurses, they would be silent. It was said at the clinic that the staff was there "in order to learn": the Professor was lord and master, he could use whatever tone he pleased—and also teach it to others.

Fine, let him!

With regard to the things I have mentioned, the Professor could perhaps excuse himself by referring to the possible impact of certain aspects of the system. I have no interest in differing with that. One could, for example, call attention to the man's overall position as medical director at the clinic, hotel manager and host to a hundred more or less sick guests all the time, and with a vast service staff, male and female, under him. It would probably have set any other university professor's nerves on edge. And I can well imagine that some occasional severity and discipline, perhaps even a "roar," is necessary to maintain obedience in that house at Vindern.

On the other hand, the Professor will not be able to refuse blame for actions and decisions for which he is personally responsible. Among these I count his determined effort to summon my wife for interrogation and use her statements against me, recording her testimony and being cognizant of the fact that it was subsequently passed on to lawyers and office clerks in the various judicial departments. Here Professor Langfeldt has no reasonable excuse. Which my wife does have, to a high degree. She had lived for months in the silence of imprisonment, and now, feeling nervous understandably enough, she chattered away. Her listener was a great public figure. He had brought a stenographer to take down her words.

I do not think I'm complaining without reason. The Professor had repeatedly been after me for information about my "two marriages." In the end I answered not a word. The last time it was done in writing. In my brief answer—also in writing— I said about my marriage: I could scream with horror at the idea of involving any of that here, behind my wife's back, since she is just as much in custody as I am!

Wasn't that plain talk? It was not only myself I wanted to screen. But the whole enormity.

But the Professor was not at a loss: with the

134

help of the Attorney General he had my wife brought for questioning from the prison in Arendal to the clinic at Vindern. The result can be read by anyone, by the entire public, in the big dossier.

I had landed in a situation that to me had been unthinkable: to be committed for observation to a clinic for the mentally ill. Professor Langfeldt could deal with me at his pleasure—and he was greedy for pleasure.

I do believe that if he had considered in advance exactly what he had in mind to do, he might have abandoned his plan. After all, I had kept my wife and my marriage out of it for several months, and quite rightly so. Where would it all end up eventually? Would any person or anybody's family life—including the Professor's—remain intact? Usually relatives are hurt, children have to suffer; finally, there is usually a certain limit that fairly well-bred people are loath to overstep.

At the time when my wife was forced to appear, the Professor must long ago have realized that I was not insane. So what was the purpose of summoning her—besides curiosity and scandal? Is the Professor ready to claim that the observation would have taken another course without her being involved? Is he ready to claim that, without her involvement, I might have been declared insane?

The material is available. Someday perhaps it will be examined.

I think even now that the Professor's conduct was inexcusable. He could have found a more auspicious form for the conversation with my wife from the very outset. When he saw and heard where it was going to end, he could have gotten up and left the further digging in other hands, in those of the competent female doctor. He is apparently incapable of conceiving such a thought; however, the possibly rather excessive willingness that was exploited in order to squeeze out another person's many imperfections might well have made a finer psychologist suspicious. Professor Langfeldt knows in his heart that he is not very well suited for delving into and fiddling with the intimacies of someone else's marriage. He is too square and rigid, his head is full of things he has acquired through study, and those things fall into categories, whether in life or learning.

I recall a similar, though not identical, case from

one of our neighboring countries, where the professor not only stepped down but gave up his entire position in the asylum and let himself be transferred to another one.

*

Back to the old people's home.

I'm writing about trifles, and what I'm writing are trifles. What else can it be? I am a detainee housed in an old people's home, but even if I were in prison I wouldn't have had any bigger things to write about, maybe lesser. Prisoners can only write about the perpetual everyday events and wait for their sentence, they have nothing else to do. Silvio Pellico[40] sat in an Austrian prison and wrote about the little mouse he had adopted, his adoptive mouse. I write about something like that—for fear of what might happen to me if I wrote about something else.

We have, among other things, a certain cockerel, the first time he tried to crow. It was a serious matter. He hadn't even mentioned that he was a male, for fear that someone would come and watch. He did some exquisite hocus-pocus with his throat and tried to get the feel of it. He did some even more exquisite hocus-pocus but made no headway. The poor devil was alone in the world and didn't dare take a chance. Then he heard something in his throat, it was horrible—and at that very moment he did it! The little hens crowded around and looked at him. What were they looking for? He hadn't done it. He was ashamed and had better keep quiet; nobody was going to get him to admit that he had done it. Later in the day it came over him again; he didn't deny it any longer, it was no use, it must take its course. Oh, how full of abysses the world was! Afterward he did it often.

When he was a grown fellow and still didn't understand a thing, he happened one day to tread his wing. A hen looked up. He treaded his wing once more, and the hen looked up. Was she making fun of him? There she was curtsying to him, in a flagrant tease, but that he wouldn't stand for. Suddenly he jumped on top of her and caught hold of her tuft with his beak. It turned into a serious scuffle, sending feathers and down flying. And oh dear, what an abyss it ended up in!

One evening later on he sat on his roost and slept.

Thorarin Archer[41] was going to the wars, and so on. But then a hand grabbed him and everything became dark, abysmally dark.

*

It's raining, but only slightly, and it doesn't bother me, I have an umbrella. I make my way to the shelter in the woods where I have been before. It's occupied. What's this? Sure, it's occupied.

"Martin!" I say.

"So, you recognize me," he says.

Martin from Kløttran in Hamarøy.

He is just the same as the last time. Ordinary and middle-aged, maybe with a little more hair and beard. Not ragged but mended, patched, and so darned; he carried his shoes over his shoulder and walked barefoot. His feet were so nice and clean because he had walked in the rain today.

There is nothing secretive or affected to separate us, we were old acquaintances; he addresses me formally and by first name by turns and is good-humored. "It's nice to see you again!" we say both of us, but "Thank God that I found you alive!" he alone says.

"I figured you were using this for a shelter, so I sat me down. You don't mind, do you?"

"How did you figure that?"

"I found these scraps of paper. Do you want them back?"

"No. It's only some notes I made."

"It's songs and verses or something, isn't it?"

"Perhaps, but throw it away. Have you come from the north?"

"Yes, I've come from the north this time. And I'm going north again."

"You're still wandering around the country?"

"Yes, that's putting it about right."

"And praying to God?"

"Oh yes, God is merciful. I helped with the spring planting on a farm, a wonderful place, they had an organ."

"Did you get anything for it?"

"No. Well, I got a sack of potatoes."

"Potatoes?"

"I didn't ask for anything else. That's a mighty gift these days, they barely have potatoes in any country now."

"So you read the papers? Can you read without glasses?"

"Yes, without glasses. I'm not that old. Oh yes, I read the papers too, a little. But we had several prayer meetings at that farm where I was. They sang so nicely to the organ."

"Did you read about Truman in the papers?"

"No, I didn't. Truman?"

"Yes, he's the American president."

"I have so little education," he says.

"Did you read about Kirsten Flagstad?"[42]

"Flagstad in Lofoten? Sure, I know what that is."

"But she is a great singer. She travels around every country singing."

"Oh. No, I'm afraid I know very little. Does she travel around doing nothing but singing? That must be nice."

"Yes, in great halls and churches. And many, many thousand come and listen to her."

"Good heavens! But as for me, well, I can't sing. I should've learned how and sung under the open sky. I too have received that gift from God, I can't deny it, but what I sing is not pretty, though I do know the notes. I've been sitting here looking at you—have you fixed up your galoshes?"

"Yes. But I've got new galoshes now."

"Oh."

"Brand-new ones, never been worn. They dress me up back home."

"I went by your farm, what's its name? Oh yes, Nørholm. I went by it a while ago. A big farm. But it needs to be taken care of."

"Yes."

"But there you see how perishable everything is in life when it's not taken care of."

"Yes indeed, Martin. What do you do with the potatoes?"

"The potatoes? What do I do with them? I bake them in the embers when I go around like this. They'll make many a good meal for me. Haven't you tried it?" he asks me.

"Oh sure, many times as a child."

"It's so delicious."

"Yes."

"I know of nothing better when you've walked a long way and are hungry."

"Have you been to Helgeland since last?" I ask.

"To Helgeland? Oh yes."

"I wondered if, maybe, you have heard something about that schoolmaster who disappeared in America."

"Yes. No, he hasn't been found."

"Too bad for the family that's left behind," I say.

Silence.

"What was her name, Alvilde? And two children."

Silence.

"Has she made inquiries through the Red Cross or the Salvation Army?"

"Yes, she has," he replies. "They can't find him."

"Tell me, Martin, why doesn't she just move back to Hamarøy again? There, at least, she would be with her own people."

He waits long before he answers: "She can't move back home."

"Oh."

"She got into trouble some time ago. I shouldn't talk about it."

"Trouble?"

Since he doesn't say anything I think it over and stop asking. I recognize the cautious usage from

Hamarøy when a girl had gotten into "trouble." And I sit there putting two and two together and musing to myself.

"It's all so strange," he says softly. "A little girl, oh, a little angel of God. She was sitting in the grass, but I didn't dare go any closer and frighten her. The weather was so nice and warm, and she had a shirt on and a blue silk ribbon around her neck. I never thought anything could be so pretty."

"You wouldn't have a picture of her?"

"Me? Oh no. I didn't even go in and say I was there."

"Why didn't you go in?"

"No. I only give her pain when I come. It's so sad, she thinks it's my fault that the schoolmaster disappeared, because I was the one who lent him the money for the ticket."

"Well," I say brutally, "at any rate it's not your fault that she's had a little one."

"Oh yes, she says it is," he replies. "Since I'm the one, she says, who changed and ruined her whole life on this earth."

We are both silent.

"He's lighting up now!" he says about the rain,

peering out. Suddenly the sun comes out again. He's lighting up now: it stops raining.

I feel sorry for Martin, but I don't dare show it, I pity him, he's so patched and darned. I might like to call him my brother or kin, but he wouldn't like it. There are so many kinds of destinies in this world.

"I would've liked so much to know her name," he said. "She was sitting in the grass picking at something with her fingers. It would've meant so much to me to know it at Christmas time, when I send them a few things. I could have mentioned her by name if I'd known it."

"Can't you write and ask?"

"No. But you won't believe how pretty she was. I've seen children before, and they're all of them pretty and made in God's image, it can't be denied. But she sat quietly playing by herself in the grass and had never sinned!"

His blue, slightly worn eyes grew moist.

"Who is her father?" I ask.

"I don't know," he replies shortly. "Maybe a local."

"I just thought that she could marry him, perhaps?"

"No, no, far from it. She *is* married."

"Did you ask her?"

"Me? What do you mean? Should I—? But she said herself once that she could never marry again."

"She must be getting on in years by now."

"She? No, you mustn't think that. She's just as young as ever, you can't see any change in her."

"Well, Martin, it was nice seeing you again," I say, folding my umbrella. "I've often thought of you, you are a true wanderer, you require so little, you just wander. That's your way."

"Shall we meet again, you think?"

I want to avoid a big farewell and don't answer. But I say, "Don't you ever get tired of walking?"

"No. Well, if I get tired I lie down. In God's name."

"Tell me, Martin, while I remember it. Did you know already last year when I met you what had happened in Helgeland?"

He looked away. "I shouldn't have said anything. I shouldn't have let it pass my lips."

"But did you know it already last year?"

"Yes," he says.

Think of all he has kept to himself, all he has

patiently borne. Was he cowed? He didn't seem to be, he was only peaceful and kind.

"Martin, I can't understand you. It isn't right of her to blame you for what she's gotten into. Not right at all."

"It isn't so easy for her, you know," he answers. "She isn't even a widow, or anything. And still she has to live with people."

"I see you want to take it all on yourself, but I don't understand it."

"Take it on myself? I have a good helpmeet," he says. "I go to God with all my troubles. Otherwise I would surely be in a bad way. I pray to God that he won't forsake me. You should do likewise. Think of your age."

"Where will you be going when you leave this place?"

"I'll go find my rucksack, which I left at somebody's house. I have to change and put on nice clothes for tonight, when I go to the meeting. Oh, a big house with many windows. People will be sure to come."

"I couldn't hear anything if I went there."

"No. But I'll remember you when I stand up. I

would be so happy if I really found God tonight. With an old friend. Since we're both from Hamarøy and know each other—."

It was summer and sun. We went our separate ways, but I had already decided to show up. I would sit by the door and look on.

Martin from Kløttran, you kind soul, there you go. You have a flower inside you, a tiny little flower of a sin inside you: your hopeless infatuation with a girl, Alvilde, who wouldn't have anything to do with you. But some day you will find out that Alvilde has married that local—it can't be helped, you will have to take the blow. And you will go to God then, too, and say it wasn't so easy for her.

On the way home I thought it all through more carefully. I had no other clothes, but I would remove my shirt collar, in case someone should recognize me and wonder why I, a deaf person, had come to the meeting. I would put a dark scarf around my neck, and I would leave without my staff, which was too bright yellow.

He hadn't mentioned his almanac this time, I thought. That, too, a familiar trait—it was no longer so important to have his almanac read; time had overtaken the writer and his work, new things had happened.

I couldn't ignore his foolishness, it was there, but I would rather call it his simplicity, his childlikeness. When he mentioned the little one who sat in the grass and had never sinned, he was a saint, an instrument of God, himself innocent.

I had no difficulty finding the meeting house, posters had been put up on fences and telephone poles with two names: Simon Trostdahl, Youth Secretary and Bachelor of Divinity, and Martin Enevoldsen. Both names seemed to be well known among those concerned. "Meeting tonight. Everyone welcome." There were lots of people inside and out, all the windows were open, and several were listening at the windows outside.

A small local quartet sang a hymn, and the Youth Secretary began to speak. He appeared to be an all-right person, practiced in teaching from a selected Bible verse and nimble-fingered at finding another verse if he needed to. I can't write down what he said, it may not have been much good anyway; I couldn't hear and just sat and looked on. He spoke for half an hour.

I kept an eye on Martin. He followed everything and looked happy. When the Youth Secretary stopped, he rocked his head as if things were going extremely well at this evening meeting, both the hymn singing and the speaking; he couldn't have wished for anything better. He stood up, folded his hands and moved his lips; I gathered he was praying to God, I could tell by the fact that many others at the meeting also folded their hands and joined in. Thus he entered into his devotions.

He didn't look up any Bible verse to go by, and it was by chance that he now and then placed his hand on the Bible lying on the table. But he continued to move his lips, so he must have had something to say. Good old Martin hadn't read or thought much, he could hardly take a topic and hold forth on it as other preachers did, he was as ignorant as Jesus' disciples. What he knew of religion stemmed from that great experience in his youth, when he sat in the snow on a mountain peak and had a strong light from on high shine through him. But it wasn't a light, it couldn't be explained, it was heaven itself that came down, it was God.

He used to say that he didn't speak, for that he

had no knowledge, he only prayed to God. I believe he said rightly that he had his own way. I saw shiny eyes among the audience and handkerchiefs appeared; it was not impossible that some felt a little sorry for this kind, middle-aged man who walked barefoot through the land and needed hardly any food. Verily, he was a man who could make others join him in prayer, drawing people to him; they hung on his lips and followed him with their eyes. At one moment I saw him point to a tablet hanging beside the mirror, but at that distance I couldn't read what it said. Later I saw him stop for a couple of small children who had come forward; he at once ran up to receive them, surprised and radiant. A mother must have let them down from her lap to be rid of them for a moment, but Martin didn't mind; he lifted them both up and prayed to God for them, becoming fired up and rosy-cheeked.

All this time I had had to do without the words that he spoke.

But the whole thing—yes, what did the whole thing come to? A prayer meeting for uplift, it was called, and people had had an uplifting evening. For them it was all a living reality to go by in the coming days.

When they said goodbye to one another outside, they came down to earth again and, now rather worldly, asked to be remembered to everyone at home and such. But then the Youth Secretary took the floor again, wanting to add a few words—he seemed to have discovered me all of a sudden, and it made me squirm in my shoes. He was an all-right preacher, this Bachelor of Divinity, as far as I was able to catch his words with my deaf ears; besides, his manner was very engaging.

"The unbelievers say it is an impossibility for them to believe in what we believe. They say it is superstition or, frankly speaking, our stupidity that makes us into believers. And they enumerate many things in the Bible which they cannot grasp with their reason. But goodness, there are people among us who believe as we do and who simply cannot be accused of being stupid, isn't that so? Yes, great teachers and wise men of our acquaintance—we could mention one name after another—who are second to none, not even to Pascal[43] himself. So how are we to account for the fact that these men and women come forward and bear witness in speech and writing to precisely the same faith that we have in our salvation and bliss? I do not pretend to know very much, far from it. But I can in all simplicity answer this question. It is a miracle. It is with the help of the guidance of the Holy Spirit that we attain this firm faith and certainty in our hearts. It is a wonder that takes place in us by the grace of God. I do not know if I explain it well enough, but it is certainly strange that the unbelievers continue to be totally indifferent to their own well-being. Their good sense should give them better counsel."

We were on the verge of another prayer meeting. Martin had left a long time ago.

*

Was it last year or even longer ago that I was still full of vim and vigor? I remember it like a vision. I would jump around every morning in a wonderful state of health, and if I had written a little during the night I would jump around even more, thanking heaven for being alive. I no longer do that. I'm not in an old people's home to create a stir.

For that matter, I don't know what I'm here for.

A bit of news for the twentieth time about my "case." On June 3rd I read in the papers that my case had been processed and that the documents had already been sent to the Grimstad lower court for adjudication. Some time later it said in the papers that the Grimstad court had not received any documents and that my case had been postponed until the fall.

After 1947 come '48, '49, '50—'60—.

I see a flag at half mast. Someone has died, but it's not me. It isn't anyone else among us either, we are so durable. Our daily lives rattle along, without any escapades. On the other hand, no trifle is allowed to slip past us on the sly, or else we start mumbling. We keep track of who comes in and goes out, who has whittled himself a new stick, who has bought a new mouthpiece for his pipe. And when we get on the subject of the neighbor's dog barking so badly last night, then we mumble a lot about it.

I believe I have mentioned that one of the two beauties who sat downstairs doing the bookkeeping left us last year. There wasn't anyone among us who had the power to hold on to her. But now the other beauty has also gone her way, leaving us all here. That was a blow. There is nothing to be done about it, but it's just as scandalous for all that. They were both so good about bringing me my newspapers, and they left behind a rosy smile down the whole stairway when they went away again. But no one among us has anything to reproach himself with, we did all we could vis-à-vis the ladies. We younger fellows who aren't even bedridden should obviously have had a chance, but then the ninety-six-year-old got out of bed again and spoiled it for all of us. What sense was there in that! He had even wrapped a thick woolen scarf several times around his neck because there was a little red in it.

We are sitting out on the big balcony on the second floor; it is for our use, and we make ourselves quite comfortable on it and smoke and fiddle with one thing or another. We are in a good humor and keep chattering away, for the weather is so magnificent that we have never seen the likes before. It hasn't rained for weeks and months, the grass is getting parched, there will be shortages of fodder this winter, the gardens are gasping for air, and the potato plants do not bloom.

But these are not the things that occupy us now; that was several generations ago, when we were young. To give a typical example of our current conversation, we discuss the long staircase that leads from where we are to the courtyard, how many steps it has, who can walk it without a stick, who can take two steps at a time. We have some extremely hearty fellows among us, young swains of seventy or eighty who claim they have begun to grow freckles on their noses again, just as in their youth. One of them had his birthday recently, he had gotten the lady manager to put a sharp crease in his trousers. Oh yes. But that created bad blood. He would often come swaggering along carrying a sadly worn briefcase with a zipper, as if he were here on business. A showoff. What was the sense of rigging himself out with a briefcase and jingling a lot of keys in his pocket? Such things just aren't done. And besides, shiny shoes in the middle of the week and his visored cap at a rakish angle without the excuse of Sunday or anything!

Right now he must have been boasting wildly about something, because the others wouldn't believe him, far from it; they shook their heads and laughed in his face. He ended up despising them and left.

But it didn't mean a break for life, of course, not

at all; neither side had meant any harm. At bottom the man is quite popular, he is indispensable; nobody could hold a candle to him in explaining incredible things about earthquakes and heavenly bodies and atomic bombs. When an airplane appeared, he could tell to a tee how it looked inside.

"But there aren't any people in it, are there?" they said.

"No? " he said. "Lots of people."

More scepticism: "We don't see a soul."

He threw a glance up at the plane. "Judging by its weight in the air, I'd say there are fifteen or twenty people on board."

"Ha-ha-ha! Beg your pardon, but where are those people? Have they gone to bed and tucked themselves in?"

*

I know I should do my best not to pester anybody with my speculations and whims and feelings, nor can I stand it in others. But there is such a buzzing in my head, or perhaps it is in my body, or my soul, that it buzzes so. It's not a cold that is coming on or something I can set right by putting on more clothes or taking off some. Hush, it's something very angelic, with many violins. That's it to a tee!

And shortly afterward there is something else that is to a tee. It is either verse or chaos, but it's buzzing. A nuisance to myself and others.

When I'm tired of myself and empty and good for nothing, I take to the woods. It doesn't help, but it doesn't make it worse either. I no longer hear the soughing in the forest, but I can see the branches swaying, and that alone is something to be happy about. I have this place to myself, the same one that Martin, my friend from Hamarøy, sniffed out. It's a kind of hole or cave at the foot of a cliff with a little grass and heather on the bottom. Here nobody can surprise me from the back and see what I'm doing. It's a boon for someone who doesn't hear.

*

You have such broad hands, you have so broad a hand,
you are just a working girl, pure and simple.
I've seen you in the grain field, good genius of the land,
cutting and quickly binding, to be the champion of
     the band.
And in the potato patch you were without an equal.

You leave the books alone and do not dream,
and yet, at moments, you are nonpareil, no one fonder.
For then you are so impiously tender, knowing
        in th'extreme,
so steeped in the here and now, your senses all a-swim,
so utterly rapt in life's greatest wonder.

I've seen you in a golden aura year by year,
as you bore and fostered child after child.
You mended and you built, holding off all care,
you blessed among women—God's peace wherever
        you are!
You have such broad hands, such beautiful gray hair,
and you have ever sparkled when you smiled.

Gradually, I came to think that this wasn't turning out so badly, not at all. There are many who do not write better poems. But I step out of line at the end, of course; I bite off too much, have lines left over and must leave some unused. I'm no Robert Burns. Oh, I know it well enough, I have too much or too little, become embarrassed and desperate and tear up the grass by the roots where I'm sitting.

Arild[44] will type this up, too, and include it or throw it away, as he sees fit. I don't care. I'm quite accustomed to throwing away my scraps of paper; I've been doing it for years, thrown away and restored to favor, and thrown away again. As for these latest verses, I've been sitting in my cave for three days, throwing away and restoring to favor. And I've had to keep all my wits about me when a sequence of nice-sounding but irrelevant lines threatened to upset everything.

I'm sitting with some comrades. I have just published a collection of doggerel and have been lucky enough not to hear anything about it. But then in comes Daniel and says, "There's no sweetness in your verses!" He probably thought this was news to me. But it was not. He was perfectly right. And it wasn't only sweetness that was lacking, but all too many other things as well, the whole kit and caboodle. I recognize it in others, and at times I'm moved to silent tears by the verses of others, but I cannot make them myself. I receive so many wonderful gifts from on high, but I analyze them to bits. All it takes is that I touch them, finger the pollen.

I cannot recall whether it was Kønig[45] or someone else who spoke to me about publishing the collection, but at any rate it was foolish of me. Daniel wasn't very far wrong, he just wanted to be such an aristocrat. He had been upper class all his life, he said. Everyone has something to contend with, he had that. Now he's probably dead.

And I take to the woods and make up verses, though I'm not up to it. It's an affectation of mine. I'm angry with myself about the collection, but it can't be undone. If someone began searching through it, he might come across flashes, yes, just flashes. I do remember how indifferent I felt about it; instead of sorting them out, I picked up several sheets at a time, put them in a big envelope and sent them to Kønig.

Several years later I stood in a hotel basement in Bodø[46] and burned all my verses. That was over and done with. But pardon me, many years after that I stood in a hotel basement in Hønefoss[47] and burned verses for the last time. I no longer remember the names of my hosts, but they helped me stir the fire. Selah, David says.

It's not that I want to suggest I can well afford it.

No, no. But what I burned was probably neither worse nor better than the collection. And besides— all my versifying not only occupied me but also gave me joy while I was taken up with it. There would be some good moments, there would be flashes.

*

It said in *Verdens Gang*[48] this summer that my case would come up in September. Three days later another paper said my case would not come up in September. No one knows anything, but everybody thinks it's great fun writing about it. Why not keep quiet about me and my case?

The same sunshine, the same drought. I take my daily walk around the hamlet and see everything getting parched. It's an evil miracle. The forest is in a bad way and will probably have to be replanted in part, and the heather is without flowers for the bees. Has it ever happened before? The bees alight in their old places, take a look around, buzz a little and fly home again.

I come to a steep on the way. I try to avoid this unpleasant spot and stay on the far edge. Here gravel and sweepings and rags and refuse of all kinds have been dumped over a long period; at the worst point the guard stone has also been overturned. Good. But on the way back I walk on the near side and have to risk my life. It annoys me that I'm dizzy and scared and a born coward, so today I decide to stand and look down for once. I shudder and feel dizzy, but force myself and go still closer and look down.

Well, I went too far—.

It wasn't dangerous, I didn't roll head over heels but slid down the slope on my back, like a coward. Then I stopped.

Oh, it wasn't dangerous at all; I looked around. From where I was sitting the distance to the abyss was no longer so infinitely far, the abyss not so bottomlessly deep; I exulted over the lake far below, despised it a little, ignored it. It was by pure chance that I had landed here, and I was not going to let chance win out. I pretended to be very busy rummaging in the garbage; there were some interesting things, bits of steel wire and bones and a dead cat and tin cans. If a driver should happen to stop up there on the road, he'd better not imagine I had tumbled down; I would show him I was looking for something, that I was looking for some important pieces of paper which had been blown out of my hands.

A paper sticks up from the pile, a corner of a newspaper. I try to pull out the whole paper, but without success, and I'm left with a torn-off scrap in my hand. Since I don't have my glasses with me, I cannot read it, but it seems to be in Gothic script, hence a local paper. I pocket the scrap.

Now I have to get back on the road. If a driver is up there, I won't give him the pleasure of seeing me scramble straight up the slope; I'll sail close to the wind, tack. Oh, I certainly haven't made the trip in vain, I've got a prize in my pocket: chance did not win out.

I get back to the home slightly exhausted, but that's my affair. Obviously the prize could have been bigger as well, but that isn't worth talking about. Besides, the prize may not be all that miserable once I've had a chance to examine it. It was a scrap of newspaper without beginning or end, a fairly long text, but ripped off so awkwardly that it was meaningless. As far as I could see, it dealt with a man and woman who had a wretched time of it together, a rather banal affair from Bohemian life. I could have discarded the scrap, but I wanted to get something in return for bringing it home. At any rate I had no intention of turning the episode into high drama. Here I was the one holding sway, able to do as I pleased. I could simply reconcile the two people, those nincompoops. I had the power to do it. Go home and make up.

*

"*Can't* you get that brat to shut up for once!"

"No, I obviously can't."

"So, that's all the help I get from you!"

"You try to soothe her."

"Yeah. But I simply have to finish this damn drawing. It's twenty-five kroner, you know."

"That won't even pay the rent."

"Oh, it's impossible to talk to you. You come at me at once and knock me down."

"How long have you been working on this drawing?"

"Since last year. And now I'm going to leave."

"Oh no, you won't. Because I must be off with the laundry."

"So, you go too."

"And leave the little one behind here? And now I'm going to have another one!"

"Well, what can we do about it?"

"I'm getting sick and tired of everything."

"You're not the only one."

"Yes, but just think—one more. And I'm so young."

"Listen, Olea, if I went to another paper, maybe they would give me more."

"Maybe."

"But it isn't finished."

"Then sit down and finish it. And I'll try to pacify her."

"All right. I'll cross out John the Baptist's head on a platter. It wasn't really any good."

"No."

"What do you know about it? But I'll cross it out anyway."

"Then perhaps you'll have room for a little stable and a manger?"

"What!!"

"Hssh, hssh, you frightened her."

"Yes, but Olea, are you *mad!*"

"I only meant a little corner. On the margin."

"Ha-ha-ha. But this is inside the royal palace, you see. In Jerusalem."

"Well, I know nothing about that, but it was nice the way it was. With many colors. It would be just the thing for a Christmas magazine."

"Olea, you'll be the death of me. Did you say Christmas magazine?"

"Yes."

"I never thought of that."

"No, you never think of anything. You just draw and cross out."

"I can't get it right, the way I want it. I'm an artist."

"Yes, and I do the laundry."

"So that's the humor you're in. But a Christmas magazine again—"

"That's where they pay the best."

"You're absolutely right. Where is my eraser?"

"How should I know!"

"No. But here we have only one room for everything. And I have to sit here slaving away."

"It isn't my fault, Frode."

"Shut up. Has it dawned on you that I'll have to erase the whole palace?"

"Oh no. Don't exaggerate now, as usual. There are many pretty colors."

"That's an idea, I'll leave some for that stable. Don't disturb me, let me just keep at it. Will you do me the favor of taking her into the hallway for a moment? I'll call you."—"Now come. Look, there is the stable and the manger."

"How lifelike!"

"Yes, isn't it? But the whole thing is completely wrong. I'll show you. It's inside the palace, after all, with a multitude of people. Herodias' daughter is dancing."[49]

"Well, that I know."

"No, you don't! And all those people, that multitude of people. There are kings and tetrarchs and captains of ten thousand."

"Just leave them alone. It says there was no room at the inn. Ouch, stop! There you erased Herodias' daughter too!"

"Well, yes. Away with her too."

"You didn't always say away with me."

"What's that, are you crying?"

"You could have left me alone. I wasn't running after you."

"But my dear Olea, you couldn't dance in front of the stable, you know."

"I could, too."

"Well, we'll never agree about my painting. But I'll make another picture of you with next to nothing on, only a bit of gauze and with lots of jewelry."

"It won't be as pretty as this one was."

"Much prettier. You still don't know me, I can make the precious stones blaze, burst into flame. You will have a triple chain around your neck. But now you'd better let me keep going and finish the Christmas picture first. I really should've made a new drawing, but there's no time for that, and besides there were so many pretty colors, as you said. How clever of you to quiet her down!"

"She has gone to sleep. A triple chain, no, that's overdoing it. But I would like to have large, drooping earrings."

"I'm going to draw a donkey here."

"If only I won't get too heavy. I'm going to have one more, after all."

"Oh no. Trust me. I'm an artist."

"Trust you? No, really now!"

"Then do whatever you please."

"Now we're squabbling again."

"I don't know what you're doing, but I'm busy, working away. I work early and late."

"Yes. And I work at my laundry, which we live on."

"Olea, you have a very big mouth for someone so small. Now I'll sketch out a simple family that'll be there with the donkey."

"I don't want to see anymore."

"I can't understand what you are so angry about. After all, I didn't cross out all the spectators who would've seen you dancing; on the contrary, it's swarming with people both here and there. And I'll leave three of the princes as they are, in all their finery, to be the wise men from the East. You'll like it, don't worry. I've certainly got a good start now, I've warmed to my task."

"Well, here I go with the laundry."

"No, wait a moment. I just have to add some bushes and a few cedars of Lebanon. You didn't think of that, did you? You should be able to get forty for such a big picture."

"Me?"

"Yes, there's no doubt that you'll get more than I

would. It has been like that every time. I'm too proud to stand there listening to those magazine publishers. Try *The Star of Bethlehem*, Olea. And let me take that heavy laundry of yours, poor thing!"

"Well, if you really want to."

"Sure, I do. I'll always be yours, you know, your own Frode."

*

I wanted to write about many things in these papers but haven't done so. I've had good reason to fear the worst and rather keep silent. Our life and our times can take their course as far as I'm concerned, everything can take its course without me. Here I sit.

Yesterday the flag was at half mast in this place. It wasn't I who had died, but a middle-aged man of fifty-six, and it was not a so-called accident, but an everyday and ordinary cancer. It doesn't matter. He, too, had probably had his plans, but then he was stopped.

And we superannuated people light our pipes and go on pottering with our own things.

It occurs to me that I saw the word *Snekker*[50] in

some newspaper. What is a "Snekker?" It isn't much of a word, really, it isn't much of anything, it's just there. It is so stripped and emptied that there is nothing left of its original content of cabinetmaker, it has ended up as an invention by journalists. I feel sorry about "Snekker," it was meant to be something better once. And now I'll make an invention of my own and restore "Snekker." It costs me only a word—if it is a word: *Snididkar*. There it is. Why shouldn't "Snid-idkar" be a word? Both roots are sufficiently Nordic at any rate, and put together they bring to "Snekker" a glorious fullness of reason and sense. I haven't always been so lucky with my inventions.

I believe I have used the word *man*[51]—one— and I use it without qualms. I don't know whether it is fundamentally German or not, but it is an indispensable word for us. Only journalists can do without it and instead call it *en*, "one." I never saw anything so vacuous and helpless as this "en," but I cannot use *to*—two—either.

I have seen the word *Sjalu*[52] in the papers, *Sjalusidrama*, crime of passion. It is neither Norwegian nor French, but is supposed to denote a concept, a state of mind. We have a splendid word for this concept in our own *Skinsyke.* I remember that Hjalmar Falk[53] wanted it to be spelled *Skindsyke*—yes, and why? Because the Lapps in North Sweden use a tanned calfskin, *Kalveskind,* when they pop the question. Oh, that Falk—what a philosopher of language he is when he goes off on his own without Torp! The Swedes themselves haven't bothered with the calfskin, but have the word *Svartsjuka*[54] for the concept. Just as we have *Skinsyke, Skindød, Skinhellig, Skinliv, Skinfektning. Sjalusi* isn't much of anything either in this world or the next. Only an invention.

Come to think, when all is said and done maybe it is quite indifferent how we use our language. As long as we can make do with it.

It was Ol'Hansa who had this idea, and who was man enough to explain it. "Just look at vowels and consonants," he said, "what do we need such things for, if we can do without them. It's all vanity, as the Preacher says in the Bible." Ol'Hansa has read many books and is knowledgeable in various trades and sciences, to give the devil his due. He had a little place with some land and a few animals, sufficient for himself and his family, nothing to waste but no daily want either, and no debt at the store. He managed very nicely. He was a journalist when it suited him and regularly picked up his pen, but he was also a great storyteller and talker whom we sat listening to many an evening. His worldly wisdom was to the effect that we human beings took too much trouble to learn all sorts of unnecessary things that we later had to keep track of. Let things take their course, then they fall into place by themselves. He may not have had the most logical head on his shoulders, but logic, Ol'Hansa said, wasn't really strictly necessary all the time. "I can prove it," he said.

"Good," we said. "Begin."

"My neighbor came to me and wanted to borrow a cowbell. Sure, he was welcome. But he didn't bring the bell back again, and after a year or two had gone by I needed it myself for a cow I had acquired. Finally I went and asked to have my bell back.

"'I'm a poor man,' my neighbor said, nearly crying.

"'My bell,' I said.

"'Yes, but God help me, can't you hear what I'm saying,' he said.

"Where was the logic here?

"So I went out to his cow barn and looked for the bell. I found it, all right; it was hanging on a nail and was dead, its clapper gone.

"I stood thinking things over for a moment. My neighbor had made himself understood without logic, thinking I would go to court for the cowbell. Then I was the one who nearly cried. Here I had an awfully good grip on a man, but I didn't use it, and I didn't write about him in the papers. It would never occur to me; on the contrary, I was deeply moved."

"Well, you are an exceptionally good person, Ol'Hansa, that's something everyone knows. But what was this thing about vowels and consonants which you started with?"

"All right. But that goes all the way back to my youth, to long before I was twenty years old, a mere boy. If you're asked about vowels and consonants at that age, you just turn pale and don't know. It's one of the worst things that can happen to you. You know about it by hearsay and have learned it, but when you finally answer, I just have to shake my head a little for you to start wavering and say the exact opposite."

"Let's hear."

"I had come to Gildeskål[55] in Salten on my wanderings and applied for a post with the sheriff. I didn't get it. Then I strolled about the hamlet a bit and came to a farm called Indyr. While we were talking in the parlor at Indyr the pastor's wife came in. She was young and handsome, everyone welcomed her and showed her to a seat. I got up to leave.

"'Is your name Ole Hansen?' the attractive woman asked.

"'Yes,' I said, bowing.

"'The pastor would like to talk to you,' she said. She looked at me and blushed, because she had come with this message and was young.

"The next day I went to the pastor and found him outside on a bench; he had a large straw hat on and his beard was gray. 'We are short of a teacher in a certain district,' he said, 'could you take it upon yourself to hold school for a little while?'

"'Sure,' I said.

"He had me find a passage in the New Testament, looking askance at me to see how quickly I could locate the place.

"When I had read a piece, he said, 'You're used to reading. When were you confirmed?'

"'Three years ago.'

"'You remember the commandments, of course. How many prayers are there in the Lord's Prayer?'

"'In the Lord's Prayer?'

"'Oh well, you mean it is one single prayer, and that's correct, too. Can you do sums? Nine times nine? Seven times six? It's chiefly the Christian faith you are to teach the children, of course. Can you write? Here is paper and pencil; let me see, write the word sanctification.'

"I wrote sanctification.

"'Those are not poor letters, but you've forgotten a c. No, my dear Ole Hansen, you don't know enough.' The pastor was getting up.

"To ingratiate myself I wrote more on the paper and showed it to him, several really long words. But the pastor as good as refused to look at it, he waved me away with his arms. 'You make so many mistakes,' he said, 'your spelling is extremely bad.'

"'I beg your pardon,' I said.

"I believe he was touched by my begging his pardon, so he didn't fail me right away; he asked about singular and plural, about consonants and punctuation marks.

"I answered at random, I knew nothing.

"'Vowels and consonants,' he said.

"It was terrible, I must have hit on exactly the wrong answer. He quickly gathered up his things, waved his large hat, said thank you and left.

"I sat for a moment and then sneaked away. I glanced back at the windows feeling like a broken man, no, a dog. Now, of course, he went straight in and told it all to his wife. 'And look here,' he'd probably say, 'here you can see what his spelling is like. It's the worst I've ever seen. And he doesn't have the faintest idea about vowels and consonants.'

"No, I didn't. And I couldn't care less, nobody should have to know that sort of thing. I tried to reverse the order and say consonants and vowels, but it made me no more cheerful or happy; no, it was anything but uplifting, so I came to feel the whole thing wasn't worth a spit. What was the point of such fancy stuff? It was vanity. And the parson himself had a sharp, unfriendly voice, I was daunted. By the way, his name was Daae, I recall."

"But Ol'Hansa, I don't understand—"

"What I'm trying to say? But I do. All these unnecessary things that we have to learn and then keep for the rest of our lives. Look at the journalists, the way they do it. They don't use that kind of parroted knowledge anymore, they manage without and are understood all the same. Today I saw a ramshackle easy chair which had belonged to an old college president; he sat in it till the day he died. He had kept track of his precious rote learning for seventy years, and now his children were selling his easy chair."

I have been playing the wag. I have made a nice mix of the journalists, Ol'Hansa and myself. So none of us should have anything to complain about.

*

Time marches on, we have snow and winter. Here I stop. Nobody knows how long I've sat here trying to think, but I couldn't get any further. I figured I could say something wonderful and striking about snow and winter, but I failed. It doesn't matter. I woke up one morning and discovered snow and winter, that's all. Oh, but it's not all, snow and winter are an evil as far as I'm concerned.

Just think, a season that is absolutely the only

one to be dreadful! Young girls mention it with chattering teeth, the wise ants flee several yards into the ground to get away from it. I'm none the worse for it, having good shoes, but yesterday I read a dispatch from some areas afflicted with famine, telling about children without a morsel of food, about children who had to be thawed on their mother's body or else freeze stiff.

And to all this man can say nothing, can ask no indiscreet questions. Yonder the mountains sit weighty all by themselves, the forest is stone dead, its life struck down, nothing speaks or listens, the snow just lies there nice and white, the frost refuses all equality and won't let man make himself heard.

Time marches on.

My "case" may not come up for a long time yet. The agent from the War Liability Directorate can do no more than he does; he informs me officially at brief intervals that the case—well, it hasn't yet been "scheduled." In October he hopes it will come up "this fall." In November as well he hopes, speaking to a couple of newspapers, to bring the case up "this fall." This fall! he says. They have decided to make it hibernate.

However, the agent receives a telephone call from a person he cannot very well ignore. They exchange a few words and agree that my case shall no longer be postponed. It is scheduled for December 16, 1947. One week before Christmas.

I walk about my old people's home and announce what has happened—no, I skip about to everybody telling the news.

*

The day arrives. The court is in session.

As I do not hear and my eyesight has been greatly impaired this last year, I'm rather confused; entering a dark courtroom, I can only make out something here and there and have to be instructed. Then the prosecutor speaks, and my defense attorney, appointed on the spot, responds. Then there is a recess.

I have neither heard nor seen what has taken place, but I'm calm and observe more and more what goes on around me. After the recess I get the floor to present my case. I have some difficulties because of the poor light; they give me a lamp, but I cannot see by it. I'm holding some notes in my hand but no longer try to find out what is written there. No matter. The piece I spoke, here given, follows the stenographic report.

(NB! From here on in the reporter's orthography, not corrected by the author.)

*

"I shall not occupy very much of the honorable court's time.

"For it was not I who announced in the press a long, long time, an ever so long time ago, that now the entire catalogue of my sins was to be displayed. It was someone from the War Liability Directorate who lent a hand in that, a lawyer together with a journalist. Anyway, that suits me fine. Two years ago I wrote in a long letter to the Attorney General that I would render a full account of myself and my actions. Now the opportunity is here, and I shall do my part in helping display the catalogue of my sins, properly and morally.

"In past years I have seen plenty of instances where someone was very clever in court and defended himself spiritedly with the help of trial lawyers, attorneys and pettifoggers, without making any difference. The verdict was in general little affected by all this cleverness. It was mostly determined by the district attorney's or prosecutor's brief, the so-called brief. It is a mysterious concept which I am unable to figure out. I renounce here and now the chance to be clever.

"Incidentally, I must apologize for my aphasia, which causes my words, the expression I might have to choose at random, to have a tendency to overstate my meaning, well, also to understate it.

"Anyway, I have already answered all the questions, as far as I can see. At first, police from Grimstad would come every once in a while, bringing me papers which I did not read. Then there was the hearing in magistrate's court two, three or five years ago. It is so long ago that I don't remember, but I answered all the questions. Then there was the long period when I was locked up in an institution in Oslo, where it was a question of finding out whether I was insane, or perhaps it was mostly a question of finding out *that* I was insane, and where I had to answer all kinds of idiotic questions. So I cannot make it any clearer now than I have already done all along.

"What might knock me down is solely my articles in the newspapers. There is nothing else that can be brought against me. As far as that goes, my accounts are very simple and straightforward. I never denounced anyone, never took part in meetings, wasn't even involved in black-marketing. I never gave anything to the storm troopers, or to any other branch of the National Union party, of which I'm now said to have been a member. Nothing, in short. I was never a member of National Union. I tried to understand what National Union was about, I tried to get to the bottom of it, but it didn't come to anything. However, it may very well be that I wrote in the spirit of National Union now and then. I don't know, because I don't know what the spirit of National Union is. But it may well have happened that I wrote in the spirit of National Union, that something had seeped into me from the newspapers that I read. In any case my articles are there for anyone to see. I'm not trying to minimize them, to make them more trifling than they are, it may be bad enough as it is. On the contrary, I am ready to answer for them now as before, as I have always been.

"It must be remembered that I was writing in an occupied country, a conquered country, and in that connection I would like to give a few very brief pieces of information about myself.

"We were led to believe that Norway would have a high, prominent position in the great Germanic global community which was now coming into being and which we all believed in—more or less, but everyone believed in it. I believed in it, that's why I wrote as I did. I wrote about Norway, which would now have such a high position among the Germanic nations of Europe. That I also, to a roughly corresponding degree, had to write about the occupying power, would seem only fair and square. I couldn't expose myself to falling under suspicion—which, as it turned out, I did anyway, paradoxically enough. I was constantly surrounded by German officers and soldiers in my house, even at night, yes, many times also at night, till daybreak, and occasionally I couldn't help having the impression that I was surrounded by observers, by people who were to check on me and my household. Twice (as I now remember), twice I was reminded by a relatively high-ranking German that I hadn't done as much as certain named Swedes had done, and it was pointed out to me that Sweden was a neutral country, which Norway of course was not. No, they were not particularly pleased with me. They had expected more from me than they got. So when I sat and wrote under these circumstances, in this state of affairs, it is easy to understand that I had to strike a balance to some extent, considering who I was, a man with a certain name, that I had to strike a balance between my own country and the other one. I do not say this to excuse or defend myself. I do not defend myself at all. I offer it in explanation, as a piece of information to the Bench.

"And no one told me that what I was writing was wrong, no one in the entire country. I sat in my room alone, thrown exclusively upon my own resources. I didn't hear, I was so deaf that nobody could have anything to do with me. They knocked on the stovepipe from down below when I was to come down for my meals, that sound I could hear. I went down, had my meal, went back up to my room and sat down. For months, for years, during all those years, that's how it was. And never a hint from anyone. I was no runaway, my name was fairly well known in this country. I believed I had friends in both Norwegian camps, both among the quislings and the so-called patriots. But never the smallest hint, a bit of good advice from the outside world. No, the world was very careful to refrain from that. And as for my household and family, the occasion to get some information or help seldom or never came. Everything had to be put in writing for me, of course, and it became too much of a bother. I was left to sit there. Under these circumstances I had nothing to go by except my two newspapers, *Aftenposten* and *Fritt Folk*,[56] and those two papers never said there was anything wrong with what I wrote. On the contrary.

"And what I wrote was not wrong. It was not wrong when I wrote it. It was right, and what I wrote was right.

"I shall explain. What did I write? I wrote to prevent Norwegian youths and men from acting foolishly and defiantly vis-à-vis the occupying power to no avail, bringing only death and destruction to themselves. That is what I wrote, in many different variations.

"Those who gloat over me now because they have

been victorious, victorious on the face of it, superficially, were not, like me, visited by families, from the smallest on up, which came crying for their fathers, their sons and their brothers who were incarcerated behind barbed wire in some camp or other[57] and had now been—sentenced to death. Yes, sentenced to death. Well, I had no power, but they came to me. I had no power at all, but I sent telegrams. I addressed myself to Hitler and to Terboven. I even used roundabout ways to contact others, for example, a man named Müller who was said to have influence and power behind the scenes. There must be an archive someplace where all my telegrams can be found. There were many of them. I sent telegrams night and day when time was short and it was a matter of life and death for my countrymen. I got the wife of my farm steward to call in my telegrams, since I couldn't do it myself. And it was those telegrams that in the end made the Germans a little suspicious of me. They regarded me as a sort of mediator, a slightly unreliable mediator they had better keep an eye on. Hitler himself finally asked not to be bothered by my appeals. He was fed up with them. He referred me to Terboven, but

Terboven did not answer me. To what extent my telegrams were helpful, I do not know, just as I do not know whether my short pieces in the papers had any deterrent effect on my countrymen, as I had intended them to have. Instead of engaging in this business with the telegrams, which was possibly quite fruitless, I should perhaps have gone into hiding. I could have tried to slip across the border to Sweden, as so many did. I wouldn't have been lost there. I have many friends there, I have my big, powerful publisher there. Or I could have tried to get myself over to England, as so many also did, who later returned from there as heroes because they had left their country, deserted their country. I did nothing of the sort, didn't budge, it never even occurred to me. I believed I could serve my country best by remaining where I was, running my farm as best I could in the midst of those hard times, when the nation was short of everything, and for the rest using my pen in behalf of that Norway which was now to obtain such a high status among the Germanic countries of Europe. This was a thought that appealed to me from the very beginning. Even more, I was carried away by it, it possessed me. I'm not aware of it ever leaving me during all the time I was sitting there in solitude. I thought it was a great idea for Norway, and I think even today that it was a great and good idea for Norway, well worth fighting and working for: Norway, a bright and shining independent country on the outskirts of Europe! I was in high favor with the German people, just as I was in high favor with the Russians; these two powerful nations took me under their wings and did not always turn down my petitions.

"But what I was doing went awry, yes, it went awry. Quite soon I found myself in a muddle, and the muddle grew even worse when the King and his cabinet voluntarily left the country and put themselves out of action here at home. It swept the ground from under my feet. I found myself floating in midair. I had nothing definite to go by anymore. So I sat and wrote, sat and telegraphed, and brooded. My state of mind at that time was one of brooding. I brooded over everything. I would, for example, remind myself that every single great and proud name in Norwegian culture had first gone through Teutonic Germany before becoming renowned throughout the world. I was not wrong in thinking that. But I was faulted for it. For this too I was faulted, though it is the most obvious truth of our history, our modern history.

"But it didn't get me anywhere, no, it didn't. On the contrary, it brought me to the point where, in the eyes and hearts of everyone, I was betraying the Norway that I wanted to raise up. That I was betraying it. Well, never mind. Never mind what all those eyes and hearts everywhere are now trying to charge me with. It is *my* loss, one I shall have to bear. And in a hundred years it will all be forgotten. Then even this honorable court will be forgotten, totally forgotten. In a hundred years the names of all those present here today will have been obliterated from the face of the earth and be no more remembered, no more mentioned. Our fates will have been forgotten.

"So when I sat there and wrote as best I could and sent telegrams night and day, I was betraying my country, they say. I was a traitor, they say. Let that go. But I didn't see it that way—I didn't feel that way, nor do I feel that way today. I am at peace with myself, my conscience is quite clear.

"I have a fairly high regard for public opinion. I

have an even higher regard for our Norwegian judicial system, but I do not regard it as highly as I do my own consciousness of what is good and bad, what is right and wrong. I'm old enough to have a rule of conduct for myself, and this is mine.

"During my rather long life, in all the countries where I have traveled, and among all the ethnic groups I have mingled with, I have ever and always preserved and upheld *the homeland* in my heart. And I intend to go on keeping my fatherland there, while I await my final sentence.

"I thank the honorable court.

"It was only these few simple things I wished to express on this occasion, so as not to be as dumb as I am deaf all the time. It has not been intended as any defense on my part. What may have sounded as such is only due to the content of my talk; it is due to the fact that I had to mention a number of facts. But it has not been intended as any defense, and consequently I haven't said a word about my witnesses, of which I may have several I could have referred to. Nor did I feel inclined to mention all the rest of the material that I have. It can wait. It can wait until another day, until better times perhaps, and for another court than this one. Tomorrow is another day, and I can wait. Time is on my side. Living or dead, it doesn't matter, and above all it doesn't matter to the world what happens to the individual, in this case myself. But I can wait. And that's what I expect to do."

*

After my talk the prosecutor spoke, after him again the defense attorney. Once more I sat for hours on end not knowing what was going on. Eventually I was handed a couple of written questions by the court, and I answered them.

The day went by. Evening darkness came on.

It was over.

*

Some mail arrives, letters and telegrams, I put it all in a pile to open later. Some days go by, Christmas is here, I move home to Nørholm and see everything again. How strange to see it now, the hills covered with snow, the bay iced over, and the old sky arching over it all as before. Commonplace, but still strange to me.

After the verdict a quiet time ensues; there is the transcript of the proceedings and the appeal to the Supreme Court. As before, there will be a wait; to be sure, nothing is going to happen for a long time to come, but we have gotten further, one step further.

I have resumed my daily walks from my days in the old people's home. I walk a comparable stretch of road to what I did then and in a comparable amount of time: from Nørholm to the bridge over the canal and home again—one and a half or two hours. It's no fun to walk for the sake of walking, but nothing else is any fun either. I'm no good at working with my hands anymore, I should have been dead long ago. What am I waiting for?

I have Arild take care of old and new mail; he sends thanks here and there abroad and throws away the rest. I don't count on having many mourners at my graveside.

In that connection: I'm not to be buried, by the way, I'm going to be thoroughly burned up, every scrap—with thanks to the Lord for the life I got to live here on this earth!

Here I could use a good opportunity and express my opinion of cremation in general. I have books—oh, I could have been diligent and found out a lot in my books about cremation. Why don't I do it? For the reason that I cannot get hold of my books. I have them within reach, but I cannot get to them; they are in their own building at the foot of the hill, and this year the road leading up to it is blocked by snow and winter. What a state of affairs!

Am I just indulging in idle chatter? Can't I have someone drive the snowplow down to the building? I shall be thorough and precise and explain myself: The men have other things to do, the horses are to haul manure up to the big bogs; it's a long way off, and slogging through snowdrifts several feet high for weeks and months makes for heavy going. I could have someone drive the snowplow, to be sure, but that wouldn't be the end of it; there is a slope leading up to the building, and that would have to be cleared by hand. Even that is not all: there are also the steps, big stone steps covered by snowdrifts several yards high, and those steps are without handrails and dangerous on several sides, and I suffer from vertigo and hardening of the arteries.

Have I explained myself now?

It's different in the summer, then I can trip lightly up the steps, for then there is no snow to blur my vision.

Nor is my vertigo a pretext. I've suffered from dizziness since childhood; it hasn't done me much harm, but has merely been something of a nuisance. Reading about tough guys clambering about on church spires, I grin and bear it sitting in my chair. I lay beneath the Eiffel Tower and held on tight as I watched the elevator make its way to the top. When I climb or descend a flight of stairs, I have to face right and left by turns. It has nothing to do with decrepitude, I was like that for eighty years before I became decrepit. Dear me, how simple all this must be to a medicine man! I had an elder brother, a devil of a fellow on the dance floor and all in all a regular guy; only, he couldn't stand the least bit of altitude. He would grow dizzy when he had to bring the sheep down from the hills in the evening. It was too high up for him. Otherwise he was quite all right. He died hearty and mentally alert at the age of ninety-one.

*

Mild weather and cold by turns, but night frost all along. Nothing to complain about. The Nørholm Bay breaks up and freezes over again, and finally it freezes over for good. It's January 13, the last day of Christmas, and the winter season is underway. Dark and short days, the newspapers empty for months on end, the breath of man and beast blows like smoke and steam out of their mouths.

Then the time comes when three grown men walk onto the Nørholm ice pulling a sleigh. They stop when they do not dare venture any further, chop holes in the ice and start fishing. They sit there until their bodies ache, sit until the dusk of evening, smoking, freezing and hanging tough. Now and then they go into their pockets with numb fingers and retrieve a crust of bread for themselves. Should a tiny little thought enter their lazy minds, they do not make use of it and do not need it; they are patient and empty, they are plump with nothing.

Then they get up to go home.

They do not like to display their catch. Only one of them has the gift of the gab: if I ask him a question he replies reluctantly; if I peek down at his sleigh he says, "Why, it's nothing worth looking at." It's as though they are ashamed, which may not be so strange: three grown men, three days' work, and these wretched little fish cadavers.

"Well, that's not bad at all," I remark on their catch, false through and through. "It could've been worse."

"We're used to both worse and better," says the one with the gift of the gab.

His companions go on, annoyed at his having anything to do with me.

"But isn't it cold out there?"

"Oh sure. But that can't be helped."

"No."

"Well, you see," he says, "a meal of fresh fish is a great help for us."

Oh dear, I hadn't thought of that. And I feel ashamed and remorseful. The family. The children.

"Aren't you coming?" the others call, turning back.

I look at them. I can just make them out in the dusk: they are mere youths, they have no family or children.

*

Curious how people manage to enjoy themselves in a world buried in snow—what cheer grown-up people, their teeth chattering, can find on the road—.

A lady appears in front of me on my walk to the bridge. I hadn't noticed where she came from, whether from a side road or from one of the houses, but she was wearing a dark coat and rubber boots, and it was a relief for my eyes to have this person in front of me as a marker in the midst of that insane whiteness.

At last, after a long while, she stopped. As though she was tired of having me behind her. When I was about to walk past her, she held up a camera (or whatever it's called) and wanted to take a picture of me.

I shook my head.

She smiled and begged sweetly, a sort of pathetic look on her face.

"I can't?"

"No—I've been portrayed enough in my day."

"I'm waiting for a bus," she says, "but there isn't a single place to sit here."

I slip off my jacket and spread it on the snow-covered shoulder for her.

"No—are you crazy!" she cries. "Will you, please, put your jacket back on right away!"

"All right. Anyway, it's warm," I say. "Only, I couldn't find my straw hat when I left."

"I think it's a few degrees of frost," she said. "Well, I never!" she said, biting her lips and looking at me.

"Are you headed for town?" I asked.

"Won't you let me take your picture? I would so much like to have it."

"Are you from a paper?"

"Me? No, no, not at all. It's just that you were walking behind me for so long—"

"I see so poorly, and it felt good to have you in front of me."

"So that was why."

"Is it the snow you're making portraits of?"

"Well, yes. The snow on the trees. It's pretty."

"That must be your bus coming, miss."

She merely looked up and let the bus go by. But at that moment she apparently seized her chance to snap a picture of me.

That was really being a bit too clever, and I said, "That you can bring yourself to do it!"

"Bring myself to do what?" she asked innocently.

I feared there would be more cleverness, said goodbye and walked past her.

When I came back from the bridge she still had not gone. She came closer, wanting to be heard: "You've just been to the bridge, haven't you? You go there every day. *You* can bring yourself to do that. You do your thing, I mine."

She no doubt wanted to pay me back, and I'm afraid I took the bait. "While you're busy with your child's play here, there are people in Europe not so far away who are dying of hunger. Do you know that?"

"I have read about it," she said.

"You have read about it."

"Well, what else can we do? What do you do yourself? Let me hear."

I had to hold my peace and look down, down at the ground. I can't say whether I moved my lips to form a word for myself and for the other guilty ones. We are all so guilty. We are millions of guilty ones, of debtors.

A bus honks, she waves at it and gets in. It turns out she was not headed for town—no, no, she rode back the same way she had come!

What was it, then, that had stirred inside her? Nothing. And what about our own flimsy little idea of playacting on the road?

She was probably a journalist or something. I haven't seen her since.

*

Open waters.

It's March. And after the marvelous weather in February and March the Nørholm Bay has already started to break up. And more things than that are breaking up—why, the ice is breaking up inside people! Grundtvig[58] is right: "As children of light we feel that now the night is over." Don't we notice a bustling life in our crumbling ruins? We heard often enough last winter about the vultures gathering over our home, good old Europe. Yes, indeed. But didn't someone hear the graylag geese early this morning? Spring is on the way.

An old almanac falls into my hands from a bundle of printed matter. There was nothing on my part that called forth this almanac from the darkness; I began turning the pages, but I paid little attention. Some way into it there is the name Verner von Heidenstam.[59] Good, I go on turning the pages. Stop a moment, what did it say about Heidenstam? I go back and read. We were the same age, born the same year, and we are both dead. And though only one of us became a specter on Gallows Hill, we both served the same goddess in our happy days. But now we are dead.

I turn many pages at a time and finish with the almanac. Way into it there is Schiller. He was born the same year as we, only a hundred years earlier. He died.

Napoleon appeared before Goethe. Did the world feel a jolt then? No. They talked together, but Napoleon had little time. When he came out again he is supposed to have said in praise of Goethe, "What a man!" That was all. It was as though they had never met. But they, too, died.

And why shouldn't we die?

Tacitus thinks that we Teutons are good at dying. And the Vikings didn't put us to shame in this respect. Our more recent knowledge makes it clear to us why there is death at all: we do not die in order to be dead, to be a dead thing; we die so that we may pass into life, we die into life, we are part of a plan. This same Tacitus praises us for not making a fuss about the grave. We merely throw some pieces of sod on top of us because of the smell. Furthermore, he praises us for not wanting to have tall monuments on our graves. That we disdain, he says. He didn't take into account our modest little decline in recent times.

*

Open waters and signs of spring. The power rationing at night has come to an end, I can wake up whenever I like and read, a great gift and blessing from heaven. Since I'm deaf and don't hear anything, I do not perceive melodies or music within me, but I'm tingling with life and joy and have many bright ideas, ho! For example, we shouldn't shoot grouse during its courtship display. We humans should not do that, it's an evil and foolish deed. Maybe so, I admit, but in any case it has nothing to do with my next random thought: I once came to a chapel, or whatever it is called, a Mohammedan temple, but so tiny and dilapidated. A tall man with a red beard was putting some rags on the ground, and on top of the rags some small stones. Then the man threw himself on his knees. It dawned on me that he was praying to God. Why did he move the stones back and forth on the rags? I didn't understand a thing, but I held back and didn't smile.

I happen to remember that I went to communion in church once. It was when I was confirmed. The parson put something into my mouth, and then he let me take a sip from a glass. There were many people around looking on, but they held back and didn't smile.

Why recall that now? I don't need it for anything, and there's no wisdom in it. It just takes up my time, because I'm happy and tingling with life. Whims, I believe it's called.

A recollection from my first period as an emigrant comes back to me. Well, nothing great or curious, merely a number of simple experiences from day to day in a foreign landscape and a small dry prairie town. There wasn't even a river, and no woods, only a bit of scrub. It went well enough, I was working on a farm for decent common people, but I was plagued by homesickness and often cried. My mistress smiled indulgently, she taught me the word "homesick."

After I had worked there a few months, the Lovelands couldn't afford to keep me any longer. We were loath to part, and it was late in the day when I set out for town. I was in no hurry; there was no road into town, only a path, and I sat down every once in a while to daydream. When the water flowed under the ice, it was not like at home; the little pulse beat under the ice was nicer and bluer back home. Then I cried a little again.

I heard footsteps on the path. A young girl. I knew her, she was the daughter of a widow in the neighborhood. The widow had asked me a couple of times to work for her when I quit at the Lovelands.

"Hello, Noot? Did I frighten you?"

"No."

"I'm going to town," she said.

She was carrying a churning stick that had come off the handle. I offered to carry the thing; I knew it well from my childhood at home, and I could easily have hafted it onto the handle with my pocketknife if I'd had a piece of dry wood.

She chirped and talked the whole time, and I had to try to answer with the few words of English

I knew. It was very irksome, and I wished she were deep underground.

"Whew, it's still a long way to town, isn't it?"

"Yes, I hope so!" said the little vixen, laughing. She didn't mind going on chirping.

We came to Larsen's workshop in town. It was getting dark.

"Noot, dear, now you'll have to walk me back," Bridget said.

"What!" I said, all agape.

"It'll be too dark for me to go by myself," she said.

Larsen was a Dane, he too said I had to go with her.

And so we started on our way back. It grew darker and darker, and finally we had to walk hand in hand and look out for twigs hitting us in the face. But it was a sweet hand to hold on to.

"We forgot the churning stick!" I cried of a sudden.

"It doesn't matter," Bridget answered.

"It doesn't matter?"

"No. I got you to come with me!"

Why did she say that? I couldn't help thinking that she was stuck on me—in fact, that she was crazy about me.

When we arrived I wanted to turn back at once, but they wouldn't let me; I must get something to eat, have supper with them, and then stay overnight. Bridget showed me a cubbyhole with a bed. In the morning mother and daughter persuaded me to settle down and work for them a little while, and I looked around the farm a bit. There were two mules and three cows. "There's no help to be had," the widow lamented. As for me, I wasn't used to working on my own; at the Lovelands' the husband was alive and could guide me, but here it was up to womenfolk to show me what was most essential. Obviously I couldn't just loaf; I chopped a big pile of firewood, and then I set about carting manure with the mules. One day followed another.

But the widow no doubt realized that she had to look around for better help, and one day she went to town herself and brought back a Finn, an able fellow by the way; he hailed from Österbotten[60] and knew his things. Young Bridget no longer seemed so happy about having got hold of me; she didn't even look at me anymore, or hold my hand.

Me oh my, what an innocent I was! But never again in this life would I trust a woman's word.

There continued to be a great shortage of workers. When I got back to town a farmer stopped me in the street and wanted me to come with him. He must have seen by my clothes and other things that I was a newcomer; I was in great demand, and no mistake. I went with the man—he was driving a carriage and pair—and when we got to his place he put me to work right away. I was to dig a little grave by the edge of the forest, he gave me the measurements in feet. It took me no time at all, and when I was through the man came out with a little coffin on his shoulder and placed it in the grave. That didn't take any time either, and when I waited for new instructions he motioned me to fill up the grave and cover it with sod. Then he left.

But good heavens, wouldn't he come back? No. He was doing something in the outbuildings and seemed to be very busy.

I was surprised, shuddered and felt unhappy. A dead child had been buried, that was all. No ceremony, not even a hymn. The people I had come to were young, but I couldn't speak and didn't find out what denomination they belonged to.

Otherwise I had nothing to complain about. Everything was well cared for—the house and farm, horses and cows, nice fields, no children. My duties were clearly spelled out: the man himself milked and looked after the animals, I worked in the fields; and then there was my mistress, round and fat and laughter-loving. She taught me many English words and gave me a small room with a window and a bed to live in. Curious people; they hit on the idea of weighing me on a steelyard, but I caused the spike to break loose and the steelyard came down on my head. I couldn't make head or tail of the whole thing, but they made a fuss over me and boasted of me because I was so heavy. When my mistress went into town with butter and wheat to do her shopping, I was occasionally ordered to drive her.

When the spring planting was over, the man wanted to hire me for a longer period, and I stayed till after the harvest. This must have been around 1880 or '81.[61] I was getting to feel more at ease and becoming used to the people. They were both of German descent and were called Spear. We gave each other an honest handshake when I went away.

Then I was waylaid by another man, who offered me work for the entire winter cutting railroad ties.

I didn't dare accept the offer. The man then offered to lease me his own little farm. Since that didn't interest me either, he tried to sell me on credit a couple of horses and a wagon for carrying freight. He was full of expedients and speculations, and I had trouble getting rid of him.

One day in town I was offered a job in a store as delivery boy. That offer I accepted. I carried packages and boxes around town according to the addresses, and after completing my run I returned to the store. It was the biggest local store, with many clerks behind the counter. The owner was called Hart and was an Englishman. We sold all kinds of things, from green soap to silk fabrics and canned goods, from thimbles to writing paper. Here I just couldn't avoid learning the names of all our merchandise, and my vocabulary received a gratifying boost. After a while my boss decided to give my job as delivery boy to someone else and let me have a permanent place behind the counter in the store. I was now wearing a white collar and shiny shoes, had rented a room in town, and dined at one of the hotels. The farming folk whom I had come to know previously couldn't get over their surprise at my rapid rise in the world. Young Bridget from the farm also came to the store and noticed my new status; now she would probably feel sorry to her dying day that she had broken up with me. I don't know.

I understood quite well that she would like to get me outside and talk to me. She said, "Noot, dear, would you please help me with my parcels?"

"With the greatest pleasure!" I said. I could easily have given the new delivery boy a hint to do the job, but I said, "With the greatest pleasure!"—a wonderful reply. Then I personally carried her parcels out to the wagon, brushed the dust off my clothes afterward, and inquired politely about the farm and her mother and the Finn. Well, the Finn had left and the crops were all harvested. But now her mother didn't want to slave away at farming any longer; she planned to sell out and move into town to open a business in chocolate and cakes and soft drinks. Young Bridget was delighted; they had already picked out a small ramshackle place for their restaurant, a shack that could be fitted up for this purpose.

Here my friend Patrick enters—Pat, an Irishman, somewhat older than I, an adventurer, comrade, and a character. Pat, like me, lived in a little attic room in town. We often talked and suffered from homesickness together, and shared a desire to get back home as soon as we could afford it.

Pat may have done some construction work in his homeland and had nothing against being called an architect. He sat figuring out the restaurant in terms of feet and inches, making a point of getting it right. He had supplied himself with planks and boards, and in my store he bought nails and tar paper. And so he kept at it tirelessly.

We had a great deal to do with one another and met every day; now and then we might have a dollar that the other one needed, and we lent each other books. Ah, but our mutual book lending didn't amount to much: I didn't know enough English to read Paine's *Age of Reason,* and he didn't understand J. P. Jacobsen's *Marie Grubbe,*[62] which I had ordered from Chicago. Those were days of youth, groping and hard-working. But we never forgot that we wanted to get away from this country and return home; and we would cry in private and feel sorry for ourselves.

How could Bridget keep from throwing herself

on the ground and wailing when her childhood home was sold! There was, after all, a little path into the woods, and in the trees in the woods there were songbirds which were now abandoned. And besides it was spring, and there were flowers and heavenly rain and a soughing in the grain field on summer days; had Bridget forgotten that? And the brook that flowed so sweetly down through the whole field—now it's sold. Good Lord and Father, the brook is sold! And the farmhouse ruminates and understands what has happened, the unpainted plank wall looks back at her. She should have laid her cheek against that wall and never gone away from it.

"We don't understand the people here," Pat says. "That's what makes it so unpleasant for us. I worked last year on a farm in Wyoming. The man would frequently pore over printed flyers and pictures that he received in the mail; one day he came up and said, 'I'm leaving!' Then he took his family and went to Florida. Gave up his farm in Wyoming and went to Florida."

"No, Pat, we don't understand the people here. We have to get away."

"But Bridget is a sweet girl," Pat says.

"What do you mean by that?" I ask.

"She's a sweet girl. I'm doing some work for her and her mother now. You don't know Bridget. They are starting a restaurant."

"So that's it!" I say.

But from that day on I began to have my doubts about Pat and his longing to return to his homeland. We talked about it and discussed it. Sure, Pat said he was still just as eager to go home again to Erin and enumerated all its glories and delights. There were miles and miles of green meadows with cattle and sheep, and churches and castles too many to count.

I sat and listened, nodding to indicate that we had the same things at home.

But Pat tasted blood and claimed that no other country could match Erin, with its long mountain ranges that went through ten or twenty counties right out into the Atlantic. And great rivers and cities and lakes with ships, and processions with the cardinal at the head.

I nodded to much of this and said that we had the same things. But the upshot was that we each sat there bragging about our own homeland. "Mt.

Galdhøpiggen," I said, "Mt. Lomseggen.[63] At Mt. Lomseggen there is a church, and in that church I was confirmed in 1873," I said.

This, which would melt a heart of stone, did not move Pat. He had tasted more blood and talked wildly. He mentioned an Irishman who had invented a machine that could fly in the air. Yes. And he told tall tales about the basalt caves in Antrim[64]— he was himself from Antrim, he said, and the caves reached all the way to the center of the earth. Sheer frenzy, that is, exalted patriotism. He expatiated upon his olive groves and rose gardens and upon the fly fishers sitting shoulder to shoulder along every river—.

"Ha-ha-ha, fly fishers!" I said. So he hadn't heard about our fisheries, had he, about Lofoten and Finnmark?[65]

"No."

"In addition to all the other things we have." Were our great forests and our waterfalls worth nothing? "Shut your trap, Pat!" Wasn't it a fact that we discovered America five hundred years before Columbus? And wasn't it a fact that our borders even today went all the way to Russia?

"To Russia?" Pat said, disbelieving me.

Oh, well. Still, the main thing was that we both pined for our homelands. But I had my doubts about Pat.

Doubts about Pat? Wasn't he suffering hardship here and living in an attic with a little kerosene lamp for lighting? If only his folks knew—yes, if only his father and mother knew! But he hadn't wanted to write and tell them. He who back home had two riding horses in the stable, while here he had a slanting roof with a tiny one-pane window in an iron frame to push open.

"Do you really have riding horses back home?"

"You are surprised, aren't you? Do you know how many windows there are in our main building? Many more than in the whole town here. And when I stick my head out through the roof, I see nothing but clotheslines in the yard. You have no idea how exasperating it is for me to watch those crisscrossing clotheslines with their waving and flapping garments, while I have to sit up here doing my architectural work in straight lines. But I'll stick it out for Bridget's sake, for Bridget is a sweet girl."

"How are you going to get home if you tie yourself down with a girl here?"

"I'll take her with me," Pat said.

"You'll take her with you?"

"Sure. Did you think I would abandon her? Then you don't know me. I'll simply take her with me."

"That I'd like to see," I said.

But now everything began to go wrong. Indeed, it could hardly have gone worse.

The clotheslines belonged to Kleist, the baker, who also had his bakery in the yard. One night Pat went out, untied all the lines and laid them neatly to one side, but in the morning there was a great commotion. Kleist was an Austrian, a Viennese, a kind middle-aged man, but he refused to put up with this sort of prank. They had a serious talk about it and Pat explained himself: it was no prank, but a torture to him. "You can't stand looking at a clothesline?" Kleist asked. "No, I can't," Pat said. "Ha-ha-ha," laughed the Austrian, enjoying the joke. And he tied the clotheslines up again.

But it became more than a joke.

It so happened that young Bridget, the Bridget from the farm, came to the baker as an apprentice just at that time. She was going to learn to bake all the usual cakes and rolls and Danish pastries and sweets for her restaurant. It might be a smart idea on the part of mother and daughter, one that would pay off; and it did go well for a while, not even Pat found anything to criticize.

But eventually it turned out badly.

The restaurant had been opened with great success. Pat, the architect, had turned the shack into a house; there was not only a room with seats for those buying soda pop and chocolate, but also, lo and behold, an annex with space for kitchen and bakery. And upstairs there were several small private rooms for mother and daughter.

Meanwhile the baker profited by giving good advice throughout it all, but he went too far. Why couldn't he have stopped in time! He behaved too young. He had grown-up children with jobs, but he must have begun to take an interest in the handsome young girl who wanted to learn his craft and was so quick. At any rate he helped her install a big stove in the annex, with many burners and griddles, and turn the annex into a pastry cook's shop.

Fine. But the old goat began to wash clothes for

Bridget. Of course, he always had hot and cold water in his big basement, and when he washed the dough off his own baker's uniform he would also include Bridget's. He had guessed that she wasn't well off and wanted to help her. That may have been a sweet thought, but he went too far, and it made bad blood between him and Pat. There Kleist, the baker, was washing little aprons and bibs and hankies, things that couldn't possibly be his own—

And hanging them up on the clotheslines in the yard!

Pat looked me up in the store and wanted me to come with him. He was deathly pale.

"You have to move, find another room," I told him.

"You can't mean that," Pat replied. "I must have a lookout."

We went over to the baker. Pat wanted to buy the lot, but he had no money, nor was Kleist willing to sell.

"What's the matter with you?" Kleist asked. "I wash and hang the clothes up. I have to be clean and snow-white all day, don't you see?"

220

"It's all those women's things you're hanging up," Pat said. "You dirty swine!" he said.

"You can't stand seeing women's things, is that it?" Kleist asked.

"No, I can't," Pat said.

"Ha-ha-ha!" The Austrian laughed uproariously.

Incidentally, Pat was very poor at holding his own, he just stood there with trembling lips. In the end he threatened his enemy in no uncertain terms that he would get tough; he would inform his family in Erin of the matter, he said, and his family belonged to the nobility.

That didn't make much of an impression on Kleist; he looked uncomprehending, nodded and left.

"You must move," I told Pat. "You can see that this won't do."

"I won't move," Pat said.

No, of course not; he had to become even more idiotic, even more batty! I was exasperated with him and let him know it. How far did my understanding of this new side of Pat go? I saw only his comical and desperate infatuation—and nobility, what was that about? It was perhaps something grand in

Ireland, though I didn't know what. I made fun of him for being so smitten with that little farmer's daughter of his as to lose his head.

"I could die for her," he said.

That was quite something. "And you being of noble birth and all," I said at random.

"I'm not the one who is of noble birth, it's my mother," he said.

He took a letter from his pocket and showed it to me; on the back of the envelope there was a little design in green enamel which he called a coat of arms. To me, at any rate, it looked classy. Unable to understand anything, I could only keep quiet, but I felt confused. Still, I made fun of him for those two riding horses of his.

He replied, "My dear Noot, you don't understand any of these things. We have an estate, that's why I could have two riding horses."

That didn't make me understand it any better.

But from now on Pat lay with his head up through the roof hatch all day long, keeping an eye on the pieces of clothing down in the yard. He went crazy, prey to an overwhelming jealousy which he seemed unable to get the better of. I laughed at him, but it cut no ice. His eyes would become extremely sly, no one was going to fool him; more women's things might well turn up, but not a single one would escape his attention.

Completely dotty.

This went on as long as Kleist was giving instruction in the art of baking, but one day he announced that young Bridget was fully trained and could bake cakes on her own, at home in the restaurant. Then came the release.

Kleist was a good-natured old Viennese; far from being a sinister old goat, he was a master of his trade and proud of his diligent student. As it turned out, he wasn't even interested in the ten dollars he was supposed to get for his instruction, flatly refusing to accept it. He had his own good business in town and made a nice living from it. And now, after weeks and months, he became his ordinary everyday self again, and nothing had happened.

But with Pat a big change took place: he was no longer in love with Bridget. It was a miracle. And what a miracle: he was no longer in love with Bridget!

He who had been so down in the dumps, so badly

smitten, he who had recently spoken of dying for her—how was it all to be understood? It was very simple: he had nobody or nothing to be jealous of anymore, there was no longer anything to goad him on inside him, and so his passion evaporated and his vehemence wore off.

Poor Pat, he had become skinny and haggard because he hadn't had time to eat; his watch in the roof hatch hadn't allowed him to get away. But he put some muscle on his bones in a short time, lifted up his head and stood tall, Pat did.

We went together to the restaurant. Pat didn't say anything, we had chocolate and cakes and paid. Pat had no love to keep up anymore; quite the contrary, he threw out hints about needing to be paid. Mother and daughter looked up, surprised. He was so changed, there was a new side to Pat.

Paid—well, for the work, sure. But couldn't he come and live upstairs, in one of the small rooms he had built?

Pat shook his head.

But why, then, had he made those small rooms?

"I need my money," Pat said. "I'll be heading for Wyoming."

They were extremely reluctant and slow. Bridget was perhaps the worst, she had been spoiled by her fatherly friend Kleist, the baker, and had a bee in her bonnet.

I was annoyed with her, she had become too clever. She was bustling about in city clothes now, but she had seen her childhood home being sold without sorrow. No, she was no good.

"I walked past Larsen's workshop the other day," I said. "Your churning stick is still there."

"What did you say?"

"Your churning stick. You didn't pick it up."

"Well, I never—my churning stick—I have no use for it—you can have it, Noot. Ha-ha-ha!"

"Then I'll have something for my trouble carrying it, anyway," I said.

"Hssh, Bridget," the mother said.

"My work comes to two hundred and forty dollars," Pat said.

Mother and daughter clapped their hands together. "We'll get an appraisal of the work," they said; they treated Pat disgracefully. Oh, they knew what they were doing: the appraisal would take time, and Pat needed the money. Finally he had to agree to settle for half simply to get his hands on the money. "Trash!" Pat said.

Anyway, I was very pleased that he had got rid of Bridget, and there we sat again discussing our future. Spring was just around the corner, and we were anxious to get back home. For my part, I was going to quit my job in the store—I had been there more than two years, but the pay was poor and nothing came of it. Now I wanted to go west, to the prairie, where I would get my board and have no expenses while working.

"Nothing will come of that either," Pat said. "I'm going to Wyoming."

"What will you do there?"

"Look around a bit. I can sell that farm, you know."

"What farm?"

"The one I worked on."

"How is that—it wasn't your farm, was it?"

"Well, the man abandoned it and went to Florida."

Speechless, I looked at him and thought, Did that make it your farm? Pat, Pat, you are a strange character, a walking adventure, and now I'm confused about you again!

"I'm going to sell it anyway," he said.

"Then I suppose you have the right to do so," I said. "You have money coming to you at that farm, don't you?"

"Yes," Pat said, jumping at it.

"I see. You stayed around the place, working early and late, and never got anything for it?"

"Yes," Pat said.

I nodded to say I could see it very clearly. "And you were there for a long time, perhaps for years—"

"A year and a half," Pat said.

"Of course. But then there's nothing wrong, I'm glad you told me about it. Remember to give me your address before you leave."

When Pat had left it was even more unpleasant for me in town. He was an indispensable companion, and I missed him. I wrote him a couple of times but received no answer. Maybe he didn't have time, maybe he was already busy preparing his return home. Finally, toward the end of my stay in town, Mr. Hart offered me a decent raise in salary if I would stick around. It was too late.

I went to Dalrymple's Farm in the Red River Valley and remained there until after the harvest.

227

*

Today I believe it is three years since I was arrested. And here I sit.

It hasn't done me any harm, it hasn't concerned me. It happened to me by mere chance, and I don't intend to say anything more about that. I've had practice in keeping quiet.

We are all of us on a journey to a land where we will arrive soon enough. We are in no hurry, we take the chance occurrences in stride. Only fools make faces at the heavens and invent big words for these chance occurrences, they are more persevering than we are and cannot be avoided. Goodness, how they persevere and how unavoidable they are!

We have now had warm weather and summer for a long time, up to seventy-four degrees in the shade. Then suddenly it changes, and the sky turns limpid and frosty. It's night, but I go out to look into the matter. It is full moon, but there is no moon. What? It's quiet all around, not even a mosquito. Two hours later I go out again and see a rising moon over the treetops.

This may not be a major sign of disorder, far

from it, but it is certainly somewhat confusing. Had I stood sufficiently high up two hours ago, I would have seen the moon climbing up from the sea like a jellyfish dripping with gold.

Ah, those permanently impaired mental faculties of mine that are making me so stupid!

I have hardening of the arteries, of course, but that doesn't do me any harm either, it doesn't concern me. When I put on the dog to myself, I call it gout. It's now more than a year since I stopped using a staff. What did I need a staff for? It was merely a sort of swagger on my part, like wearing one's hat at a rakish angle and such. Was the staff any support to me? No. We had become companions, but nothing more. When we fell, we were always lying far apart in the snow.

As was to be expected of companions.

But naturally my gout is a terrible nuisance. I can't hear. All right. But I can't see, that's worse. I cannot read the paper anymore, a miserable newspaper. No matter. However, that too is a kind of boast; I can read it well enough when I get strong sunlight on it.

In Nordland we had something called "walking

229

sight," seeing well enough to walk. When Maren Maria Kjeldsen came walking along, she still had her walking sight, but she used a staff and had many other infirmities. Maren Maria was a mysterious figure among us; nobody knew anything about her, but people said that she had once been a fine young lady, daughter of a skipper or something, but it was only a shot in the dark, and she herself said nothing. Everyone believed that she came of good family, for her name was Kjeldsen, and no one else had that name in our part of the country. When she wandered about our neighborhood, she had only one errand: to beg chewing tobacco for her headache. She had gotten used to tobacco in her younger days and couldn't do without it anymore; she chewed her quid like a sailor. She was unappetizing in other ways too, with no sense of shame. But this woman had the most beautiful hands, like those of a young lady. I marveled at those hands: though yellowish in complexion, they were nice and soft, never used for doing anything, never particularly clean, but so beautiful to look at.

In the end Maren Maria became a parish pauper and was taken in by the farmers in turn; she must have been seventy or eighty years old by that time. She could see well enough to walk her charted route between the farms without an escort; she had her walking sight until the end.

It is a blessing to have walking sight for many years ahead.

*

Midsummer Day 1948.
Today the Supreme Court has handed down its verdict, and I end my writing.

Notes

1 Coastal town in Aust-Agder county, ca. 125 miles southwest of Oslo.
2 Coastal town situated about twenty-five miles southwest of Arendal.
3 A principal Norwegian newspaper. Founded in 1860, *Aftenposten* has since 1880 represented a conservative political viewpoint.
4 Of these magazines, published by different evangelical-Christian organizations, *For Rich and Poor,* founded in 1848, was the most widely known journal of its kind in Norway at the time, with a circulation (in 1951) of 57,000.
5 Danish author Vilhelm Topsøe (1840–81) wrote a number of psychologically insightful stories and novels in the 1860s and '70s. Topsøe opposed the radical political ideas of Georg Brandes, but accepted the latter's call for a realistic depiction of life.
6 Under the editorship of Christian Friele (1821–99), *Morgenbladet* (est. 1819) became Norway's leading conservative newspaper. From April 1943 until the liberation in May 1945, it was discontinued by order of the German occupying power.
7 Georg Brandes (1842–1927), seminal Danish critic, was the chief intellectual force behind the breakthrough of realism in Scandinavian literature. His lectures at the University of Copenhagen on Main Currents in Nineteenth-Century Literature (begun in November 1871) were later published and translated into many languages, including English (1901–05).

8 Peter Lorentz Stabel (1877–1950), a scion of several generations of lawyers, had been judge in Grimstad since 1933. A
   well-known patriot, he was relieved of his office during the
   German occupation of Norway. Reinstated after the war,
   he presided at the Hamsun hearings.

9 Josef Terboven (1898–1945) was Reichskommissar for occupied Norway from April 24, 1940 until the end of the war;
   he committed suicide on May 8, 1945. Terboven used
   Skaugum, the King's private estate, as his residence and the
   building housing Norway's parliament (the Storting) for his
   offices.

10 The figures here mentioned represent different forms of op-
   position to government authority. Marcus Thrane (1817–90)
   was the first Norwegian labor leader. In 1848 he formed a
   labor union, and the following year he started a paper. Thrane
   was arrested in 1851 and spent eight years in prison. In 1863
   he emigrated to the United States, where he worked as a
   journalist. Kristian Lofthus (1750–97) was a Norwegian peasant leader. He went twice to Copenhagen, capital of the
   Danish-Norwegian kingdom—the second time with thirty-
   six other men—to complain about the injustices done to
   the Norwegian farmer by government officials. Arrested in
   March 1787, he was incarcerated in Akershus Fortress in
   Kristiania (now Oslo). In 1792 he was sentenced to hard
   labor for life. Hans Nielsen Hauge (1771–1824) was the most
   influential Norwegian revivalist. In the eighteenth century
   official Christianity in Norway, as in many other European
   countries, was marked by the rationalism of the Enlighten-
   ment. Hauge preached the necessity of conversion and em-

phasized the importance of personal religious experience. However, his activity was seen as a threat to officialdom—clergymen being government officials—and between 1804 and 1814 Hauge was confined to prison in Kristiania.

11 Hamsun's estimate seems a bit high. At its peak, membership in *Nasjonal Samling* (National Union) was slightly above forty thousand.

12 The person Hamsun has in mind is Gerhard Smith-Petersen (1859–1933), *Officier d'Académie*, ship broker at Grimstad and French consular agent since 1892.

13 Albert Engström (1869–1940), Swedish graphic artist and author and a good friend of Knut Hamsun, created an entire gallery of character types which immortalized the everyday life of contemporary Sweden.

14 Bjørnstjerne Bjørnson (1832–1910), poet, novelist and dramatist, was a leading Norwegian writer and politician. Hamsun, who had few good things to say about Ibsen, Bjørnson's great contemporary, admired Bjørnson.

15 The word here rendered as "patriot" is *jossing*. The word derives from the Jøssing Fjord in West Norway, where in February 1940 a British squadron freed three hundred seamen held captive in the German tanker *Altmark*, which had sought refuge in Norwegian waters.

16 In strict usage, the name of the county extending ca. three hundred miles northeast between the counties of North Trøndelag and Troms; more broadly, a general term for North Norway.

17 A section of Nordland county about one hundred miles southwest of Narvik.

18 Township and parish in Nordland county, extending from the West Fjord to the Swedish border ca. fifty miles to the southeast. Geographically, the name refers to a peninsula, fifteen by seven miles in area and divided in two by the Hamsund isthmus. Hamsun, born in Lom township in west-central Norway, spent most of his childhood at Hamsund, from which he acquired his name. Between 1911 and 1917 he owned and lived on a Hamarøy farm, along with his growing family. The farm, Skogheim, was located near his childhood home.

19 The Sagfjord is the longest fjord in Hamarøy, twenty-five miles long and three miles wide.

20 Klingenberg, like most of the places mentioned later in Martin's story, is located in Hamarøy.

21 A fjord, township, and parish in Troms county located ca. twenty miles northwest of Narvik.

22 Helgeland is the name of the southern part of Nordland county.

23 Tromsø is the principal city in Troms county. It is 580 miles farther north than Trondheim, 135 miles from Narvik.

24 Hamsun was very conservative in matters of Norwegian orthography, which underwent more than one revision during his lifetime. In this instance he ridicules the attempt to distinguish Norwegian from Danish spelling of the word for "physician."

25 Ove Mossin (1850–1912) is said to have done an excellent job as head of the Kristiania criminal investigation department. However, during his subsequent tenure as Deputy Chief of Police he was criticized for his brusque, tactless manner, which caused offense and landed him in difficulties.

26 A remarkable variable star, with fluted spectrum, in the constellation Cetus.

27 Township and parish in the county of South Trøndelag.

28 Township in Hedmark county some sixty miles north of Oslo.

29 Paul Botten Hansen (1824–69), Norwegian critic, editor, and great friend of the young Ibsen, with whom Hansen and another Norwegian writer, Aasmund Vinje, published an important literary journal in the 1850s.

30 Robert Louis Stevenson (1850–94), Scottish author best known for his adventure novels, settled in Samoa in 1889 for the sake of his health. A tuberculosis sufferer, Stevenson lived there until his death.

31 Hamsun's lifelong friendship with Erik Frydenlund (1862–1947) began in 1884, when Hamsun went for an extended stay to North Aurdal in the Valdres region of Oppland county, ca. one hundred miles northwest of Oslo, to recover from the illness contracted during his first sojourn in the United States (1882–84).

32 Adolph Wilhelm Dinesen (1845–95), Danish officer and author, and father of the writer Isak Dinesen. After an international military career, he settled on a farm and published two collections of "Hunting Letters" (*Jagtbreve*, 1889 & 1892) under the pseudonym Boganis.

33 John Bunyan (1628–88), English author, was arrested in 1660 for preaching without a license and was imprisoned for twelve years. Hamsun's quotation reads like a free rendering of the first sentence of Bunyan's *The Pilgrim's Progress*

236

(1678; Part Two, 1684), which was begun during a second stay in prison.

34 The *joik* is a chant, sung by the Sami or Lapps, telling a story of a person or of past events.

35 A Hebrew word found frequently at the end of a verse in the Psalms. As for its meaning, everybody seems to know little more than the old Hamsun, but it is often interpreted as an indication of a musical pause or rest.

36 Helsingfors is the Swedish name for Helsinki, the capital of Finland.

37 Residential area in Oslo and a stop on the Holmenkollen line located a few miles from the city center.

38 An intellectually high-quality journal for politics, literature and social problems, *Samtiden* (The Contemporary) has been published since 1890, under the editorship of some of Norway's most distinguished academics.

39 Hamsun was twenty years old when he spent a few months at Øystese, Hardanger, located ca. thirty miles east of Bergen.

40 Silvio Pellico (1789–1854) is best known for his book *My Prisons* (1832), a simple, gently resigned account of life in prison. Pellico, who belonged to the secret society of the Carbonari, strongly criticized the Austrian rulers of North Italy. Arrested in 1820, he was sentenced to death, but the sentence was commuted to fifteen years of hard labor. He was released in 1830.

41 The main character in "Buesnoren" (The Bowstring), a romantic ballad by Johan Sebastian Welhaven (1807–73), which appeared in *Nyere Digte* (1845; Recent Poems).

42 Kirsten Flagstad (1895–1962), operatic soprano, was one of the foremost interpreters of Wagner. After the Second World War, she was much criticized for having sung in Bayreuth during the Nazi period, specifically between 1935 and 1942.

43 Blaise Pascal (1623–62), French mathematician and religious philosopher. After a profound spiritual experience in 1654, he devoted his attention mainly to religious writing. Pascal is best known for his posthumous *Thoughts* (1670), which argues the necessity of mystic faith for understanding the universe.

44 Arild Hamsun (1914–88), Hamsun's younger son, took over the farm Nørholm after his father.

45 This is Christian Kønig (1867–1935), director of the Norwegian branch of the Danish publishing house Gyldendalske Boghandel, Nordisk Forlag, from 1907 to 1920 and co-director of the same firm from 1920 to the end of 1927.

46 Bodø, the principal town of the Salten region in Nordland county, is located ca. seventy-five miles south of Hamarøy.

47 Small town in Buskerud county about twenty-five miles northwest of Oslo.

48 *Verdens Gang* (The Way of the World) was established as a daily newspaper in 1885. Discontinued in 1923, it resumed publication in 1945 as an independent paper.

49 Herodias, granddaughter of Herod the Great and Marianne, first married her uncle, Herod Philip, and had the daughter Salome by him. Subsequently, contrary to the law of Moses, she married his half-brother, Herod Antipas, evoking a protest by John the Baptist. Salome is generally thought to have

238

been the dancer referred to in the Bible (Matthew 14: 6–11; Mark 6: 21–28).

50 Here Hamsun expresses his irritation at Norwegianized spelling, implying that the Danish spelling formerly used also in Norwegian—*Snedker*—shows the root meaning of the word, a "woodworker." However, his suggested etymology (*snididkar*) is, as he himself admits, an invention. *Snedker* derives from the Middle Low German *sniddeker,* not from an Old Norse word.

51 The indefinite pronoun *man* is used with the same meaning as the German word. Hamsun ridicules the alternative recommended by those who believe that Norwegian should rid itself of such foreign imports.

52 Here Hamsun goes after another import, by way of French. The meaning of the verbal root *Skin* in the words that Hamsun cites is "pseudo" or "sham." The words mean, in order of mention, "jealousy" (*Skinsyke*, pseudo-sickness); "apparently dead," as in cases of suspended animation (*Skindød*, sham-dead); "hypocritical" (*Skinhellig*, pseudo-holy); "semblance of life" or "empty life" (*Skinliv*, pseudo-life). *Skinfektning* can be literally rendered in English as "sham battle."

53 Hjalmar Falk (1859–1928), a Norwegian linguist and professor of Germanic Philology at the University of Kristiania/Oslo, was a distinguished etymologist and produced, with Alf Torp (1853–1911), professor of Sanscrit and Comparative Philology at the same university from 1894 on, an etymological dictionary of the Danish and Norwegian languages

239

(2 vols., 1903–06). Falk opposed acknowledging New Norwegian as an official written language and worked for the modernization of Dano-Norwegian.

54 The Swedish word for jealousy, *svartsjuka,* means literally "black sickness."

55 Coastal township south of Bodø in the Salten region.

56 *Fritt Folk* was the chief organ of the National Union party.

57 Hamsun may be referring to the Grini concentration camp, located on a farm in Bærum township west of Oslo. Started by the Germans in June 1941, the camp had a maximum of 5,400 prisoners, mainly political, including 600 women. Altogether, about 20,000 people were at one time or another inmates of this camp during the years of German occupation (1940–45).

58 Nikolai F. S. Grundtvig (1783–1872), Danish poet, churchman, and educator. He founded the folk high school, a form of adult education designed to foster patriotism and religious conviction in young adults.

59 Verner von Heidenstam (1859–1940) was a Swedish poet and novelist. He was awarded the Nobel Prize for literature in 1916.

60 Österbotten (East Bothnia) is a historic coastal region in western Finland, with a strong Swedish-speaking minority. Vaasa is its principal city.

61 Hamsun's dates are both wrong. He did not arrive in the United States until January or February of 1882.

62 Jens Peter Jacobsen (1847–85) was a distinguished Danish poet and novelist. *Fru Marie Grubbe* (1876; English transla-

tion, *Marie Grubbe*, 1917) was the first naturalistic Danish novel.

63 Galdhøpiggen (2469m.) is the highest peak in Jotunheimen, a mountain range in the central part of south Norway. Lomseggen (2068m.), ca. fifteen miles to the north, is the highest peak in Lom township, Oppland county, where Hamsun was born.

64 Antrim is a county in Northern Ireland; Belfast is the principal city.

65 Lofoten is a large group of islands located northwest of the West Fjord; Hamarøy is on the southeast side of the same fjord. Lofoten is best known for its cod fishing (from February to April). Finnmark, Norway's northernmost county, is notable, among other things, for the cod fishing off its coast from April to June.

GREEN INTEGER
Pataphysics and Pedantry

Edited by Per Bregne
Douglas Messerli, *Publisher*

Essays, Manifestos, Statements, Speeches, Maxims,
Epistles, Diaristic Notes, Narratives, Natural Histories,
Poems, Plays, Performances, Ramblings, Revelations
and all such ephemera as may appear necessary
to bring society into a slight tremolo of confusion
and fright at least.

*

GREEN INTEGER BOOKS

History, or Messages from History Gertrude Stein [1997]
Notes on the Cinematographer Robert Bresson [1997]
The Critic As Artist Oscar Wilde [1997]
Tent Posts Henri Michaux [1997]
Eureka Edgar Allan Poe [1997]
An Interview Jean Renoir [1998]
Mirrors Marcel Cohen [1998]
The Effort to Fall Christopher Spranger [1998]
Radio Dialogs I Arno Schmidt [1999]
Travels Hans Christian Andersen [1999]
In the Mirror of the Eighth King Christopher Middleton [1999]

On Ibsen James Joyce [1999]
Laughter: An Essay on the Meaning of the Comic Henri Bergson [1999]
Seven Visions Sergei Paradjanov [1998]
Ghost Image Hervé Guibert [1998]
Ballets Without Music, Without Dancers, Without Anything [1999]
Louis-Ferdinand Céline [1999]
On Overgrown Paths Knut Hamsun [1999]
Poems Sappho [1999]
Metropolis Antonio Porta [1999]
Hell Has No Limits José Donoso [1999]
Art *Poetic'* Olivier Cadiot [1999]
Fugitive Suns: Selected Poetry Andrée Chedid [1999]
Theoretical Objects Nick Piombino [1999]
Suicide Circus: Selected Poems
Alexei Kruchenykh [1999]

BOOKS FORTHCOMING FROM GREEN INTEGER

Islands and Other Essays Jean Grenier
Operatics Michel Leiris
My Tired Father Gellu Naum
Manifestos/Manifest Vicente Huidobro
The Doll and *The Doll at Play* Hans Bellmer
[with poetry by Paul Éluard]
Water from a Bucket Charles Henri Ford
What Is Man? Mark Twain
American Notes Charles Dickens